Lady Rebels
of
Civil War
Missouri

Lady Rebels
of
Civil War Missouri

Larry Wood

The History Press

Published by The History Press
Charleston, SC
www.historypress.com

Copyright © 2022 by Larry Wood
All rights reserved

Front cover: *Order No. 11*, George Caleb Bingham. State Historical Society of Missouri, Columbia.
Back cover: State Historical Society of Missouri, Columbia.

First published 2022

Manufactured in the United States

ISBN 9781467150095

Library of Congress Control Number: 2022943543

Notice: The information in this book is true and complete to the best of our knowledge. It is offered without guarantee on the part of the author or The History Press. The author and The History Press disclaim all liability in connection with the use of this book.

All rights reserved. No part of this book may be reproduced or transmitted in any form whatsoever without prior written permission from the publisher except in the case of brief quotations embodied in critical articles and reviews.

Contents

Preface	7
Acknowledgements	11
Introduction	13
1. Jane Haller: Mother of a Quantrill Guerrilla Leader	17
2. Lizzie Powell: A Beautiful and Accomplished Young Rebel Lady	21
3. Augusta and Zaidee Bagwill: Real Good Rebels	27
4. Addie Haynes: One of St. Louis's Most Presumptuous Rebels	32
5. Lucie Nicholson: The Belle of Boonville	37
6. Hattie Snodgrass: Proud Spirit of a Southern Lady	43
7. Marion W. Vail: Confederate Mail Smuggler	51
8. Mary Susan F. Cleveland: A Veritable "She Adder"	60
9. The Blennerhassett Sisters: Uncompromising Rebel Sympathizers	66
10. Pauline White: Sentenced to Hard Labor	73
11. Martha Cassell: A Very Rank Rebel	79
12. A Guileless Escapade: Missouri Wood Buys Her Way Out of Prison	86
13. Emily Weaver: Sentenced to Hang Higher than Haman	93
14. Such a Pretty Young Lady: The Story of Jane Hancock	104

Contents

15. The Mysterious Kate Beattie: A Beautifully Formed and Highly Intelligent Woman	109
16. Amanda Cranwill: A Fair and Buxom Widow of the South	116
17. Mary Jane Duncan: Sam Hildebrand's "Sister"	122
Epilogue	127
Notes	131
Bibliography	145
Index	149
About the Author	155

Preface

War has traditionally been considered the domain of men. Certainly this was true on the eve of the American Civil War. Women were supposed to be keepers of the hearth when their men marched off to war and to welcome them back as conquering heroes when they returned. But they were expected to play little, if any, direct role in the war effort. This conception of women as apolitical beings whose lives centered almost entirely on the home was challenged by the realities of the Civil War. Women served both the Union and Confederate armies as nurses, cooks, laundresses, seamstresses, and sutlers. Some even disguised themselves as men and fought as soldiers.

In border states like Missouri that were occupied by the Union but had large Confederate-sympathizing civilian populations, many Southern women served as spies, smugglers, or mail carriers, while others fed and harbored guerrillas in the bush. Whether acting with agency and purpose to aid the war effort or merely carrying out the domestic role of feeding a loved one, the women were empowered by their covert activities, because they repeatedly clashed with Union authorities, who were forced to take them seriously. They were arrested, made to take oaths, banished, and sometimes imprisoned. These Union actions represented an implicit recognition of a woman's personhood and citizenship, separate from her identity as someone's wife or daughter. No longer could women be seen as completely outside the realm of politics.

But once peace returned, most of the Southern women readily relinquished the power and independence that the circumstances of the Civil War had thrust on them. Those who wrote about their war experiences were usually quick to reembrace the idea of man as the noble warrior and woman as the long-suffering keeper of the hearth.

Scholars and popular historians who wrote about the Civil War during the first one hundred years or so after its conclusion hardly considered women at all. If women were even mentioned, they were primarily portrayed as victims. Not until about fifty years ago did scholars begin to examine the important roles women played and the contributions they made during the war. More recently, a few historians have looked specifically at the Confederate-allied women of Missouri, examining how and why they clashed with Union authorities, how they were treated by Union officials after they were arrested, how that treatment changed over the course of the war, and how the women were affected and often empowered by their experiences.

My 2016 book *Bushwhacker Belles: The Sisters, Wives, and Girlfriends of the Missouri Guerrillas* dealt specifically with Missouri women who clashed with Union authorities for aiding guerrillas. Since its publication, other authors have continued to examine the role of women in Civil War Missouri. Of particular note is Thomas F. Curran's *Women Making War: Female Confederate Prisoners and Union Military Justice*, published in 2020. It is a meticulously researched book that stands now as the most thorough and comprehensive study of the Union military justice system in St. Louis in relation to female prisoners.

In *Bushwhacker Belles*, the main argument I advanced concerning women in Civil War Missouri was that those who were arrested only for feeding and harboring guerrillas were often motivated by family ties as much as or more than by devotion to the Southern cause. Having made that point, why would I want to write another book about the Confederate-allied women of Missouri, since I admittedly have little else to add to the subject from a scholarly standpoint that Curran and others haven't already considered?

In fact, after *Bushwhacker Belles* was published, I did not plan to write a second book about the Southern women of Civil War Missouri, even though, during my research, I found a number of women with compelling stories that I was unable to include in the book. In a few instances, their stories were left out simply because including them would have made the book longer than either I or the publisher intended. Several other women were omitted because their stories fell outside the subject of *Bushwhacker Belles*. Although more women probably came into conflict with Union authorities in Missouri for feeding and harboring guerrillas than for any other reason, many women also got into trouble for spying, distributing Confederate mail, smuggling provisions to Confederate soldiers and prisoners, and engaging in other purposeful, covert activities to help the Southern cause.

So, the answer to my question as to why I'd want to write again about Confederate women in Missouri comes down to this: I feel the stories of some of these women have yet to be told in full, and I'm a storyteller. I'm a writer first and a historian second. That is not to say that I don't strive for accuracy backed by solid research, but my focus is on human interest and not so much on historical analysis. While Curran and others have mentioned many of the women whose stories I chronicle here, they have generally considered the women collectively, briefly telling each of their stories within the context of advancing a scholarly thesis or argument. I want to tell the stories individually and for their own sake. Not that I wish to romanticize these women or promote the myth of the Lost Cause, as some of them did themselves. I just think the conflict inherent in the situations in which they found themselves during the war makes for compelling stories. I hope the reader agrees.

This book contains brief introductory and concluding chapters, with the stories of the individual women in between. Each chapter in the main body of the book chronicles the story of one woman or one group of women who were closely connected by either kinship or circumstance. The chapters are arranged in roughly chronological order by the date that the women first came into conflict with Union authorities.

Acknowledgements

Much of the research for this book was done online. Fold3.com, an online subscription service providing access to databases of military records, was my primary source. Other important online sources included the Union provost marshals' records database at the Missouri State Archives website and the census and marriage records available at FamilySearch.org. Online research such as this largely involves one-sided interaction with faceless databases that can't talk back. However, I still did a significant amount of research through traditional channels that involved the help of live human beings with actual names, and I'd like to mention a number of these folks.

I particularly want to thank Karen Needles for prioritizing several research tasks I asked her to do at the National Archives and for getting the results of that work to me in a very timely fashion once the archives opened back up after an extended closure during the COVID pandemic. I borrowed several books on interlibrary loan through the Joplin (Missouri) Public Library, and I want to thank Jason Sullivan and the rest of the reference department for cheerfully and promptly fulfilling those requests. The Missouri Historical Society in St. Louis provided a number of photos for this book and helped with a couple of research requests. I particularly want to thank Lauren Sallwasser, photo archivist, and Dennis Northcutt, reference archivist, in this regard. Not only did I utilize the online databases available from the Missouri State Archives, but I also want to thank the reference staff at the state archives for fulfilling a couple of research requests for me. The University of

Acknowledgements

Arkansas Library, Special Collections, and the Arkansas State Archives were among other institutions that fulfilled research requests, and I thank them as well. David Bollinger, president of the Wayne County Historical Society, was very helpful when I was researching Pauline White.

I'd like to thank Chad Rhoad, acquisitions editor for The History Press, for his patience and encouragement during the long delay caused by the pandemic in my delivering this manuscript. I also want to thank copy editor Rick Delaney for his excellent job of proofreading. I feel certain that his attention to detail has made this book a more polished finished product than it otherwise would have been.

Introduction

The results from the 1860 presidential election in Missouri suggest the political makeup of the state on the eve of the Civil War. Stephen Douglas, the Democrat (aka Northern Democrat) received about 35.5 percent of the vote. The Constitutional Union Party, composed largely of former Whigs who wanted to avoid secession but didn't want to join either the Democrats or Republicans, saw its candidate, John Bell, receive slightly over 35 percent of the vote as well. The Southern Democrats, who favored secession, trailed badly, as their candidate, John C. Breckinridge, received not quite 19 percent of the vote. Abraham Lincoln and the Republicans, many of whom were considered radicals because they favored abolition, fared even worse, with only 10 percent of the statewide vote in Missouri. In short, the two centrist parties received over 70 percent of the vote in Missouri.[1]

This division in political sentiment in Missouri generally held after the Southern states began to secede in late 1860 and early 1861. Although most Missourians, especially in the rural areas, had roots in the Upper South, only a small percentage of them favored immediately joining the seceding states. A roughly equal minority, called Unconditional Unionists, were unquestioningly loyal to the Federal government. The large majority of citizens, however, were Conditional Unionists. They wanted to stay in the Union but also wanted to stay out of the looming war. Adopting a position that came to be known as "armed neutrality," they said they would stay in the Union as long as the Federal army did not "invade" Missouri or oppress the seceding states, but they would resist any occupation of Missouri by Federal forces. Reflecting the ascendancy of the Conditional Unionists, delegates to a constitutional convention, called in March 1861 to decide the issue of secession, voted almost unanimously to remain in the Union.

But, of course, it was hard to stay neutral once war finally came a month later. When President Lincoln called for volunteers after the Confederate attack on Fort Sumter on April 14 and Missouri's quota was set at seventy-five thousand, Missouri governor Claiborne F. Jackson, a Southern Democrat, vowed not to furnish a single soldier. His attempt to get a military bill approved by the legislature to resist Federal encroachment into Missouri was rebuffed by moderates at first, but an affair that happened less than a month later changed the minds of many people. On May 10, a body of state militia was training near St. Louis at Camp Jackson, named for the governor. The state troops were ostensibly neutral, but Union authorities, who by now occupied St. Louis in force, suspected that the men at Camp Jackson intended to raid a nearby Federal arsenal. Captain Nathaniel Lyon, commanding the arsenal, had the militiamen arrested, and they were being marched to prison through the streets of St. Louis when civilians began protesting and throwing things at the Federal troops. In the melee that followed, almost thirty unarmed civilians were killed, including at least one

Camp Jackson on the outskirts of St. Louis, where Missouri militia troops trained in May 1861. *Missouri Historical Society, St. Louis.*

Introduction

Sketch of the Camp Jackson Affair as depicted in *Harper's Weekly*. *Library of Congress*.

or two children. The event incensed many Conditional Unionists, driving them into the secessionist camp. Indeed, some historians have observed that if the vote on secession had been taken after the Camp Jackson Affair, Missouri may well have voted to leave the Union. It was too late for that, but Governor Jackson now readily got his military bill passed, creating the Missouri State Guard to resist by force the "invasion" of Missouri by the Federal army.

The Missouri State Guard won early battles against the Union army at Carthage in July and Lexington in September. More notably, the state guard also teamed up with Confederate forces in August to defeat the Federals at Wilson's Creek, where Lyon, now a brigadier general commanding the Army of the West, was killed. By late 1861, however, Confederate forces had retreated from Missouri, and the Missouri State Guard, pinned down in southwest Missouri by the Federals, was disintegrating. Its commanding general, Sterling Price, and other high-ranking officers joined the Confederate army.

While many rank-and-file soldiers followed Price into Confederate service, many others balked at such a mission. Some simply returned home at the expiration of the six-month enlistment period they'd signed up for at the beginning of the war. Many others took to the bush to wage an unconventional partisan warfare, continuing to resist the Federal occupation of the state.

With so many men away in the Confederate army or else roaming the countryside as guerrillas, many Southern women in Missouri were left to fend for themselves, and it was almost inevitable that some would come into conflict with Federal authorities. A significant number of Missouri women with no relatives in the Confederate army or among the guerrillas still held strong Southern sympathies, and some of them were likewise destined to clash with Union authorities. Since the Union had placed Missouri under martial law in late August 1861, these women were subject to military justice. Their punishments ranged from the death penalty (although it was never actually carried out) to no punishment at all. Many were required merely to take an oath of allegiance before being released. But few, if any, of the women whose stories are chronicled in the following chapters got off that easily.[2]

1

Jane Haller

Mother of a Quantrill Guerrilla Leader

Twenty-year-old William Haller (aka Hallar) became one of William Quantrill's first recruits when he and seven other young men joined the Confederate guerrilla leader's fledgling band in Jackson County, Missouri, in late 1861. Just weeks later, the small force had grown to about thirty men, and Haller was made first lieutenant, second-in-command to Quantrill. John N. Edwards, Quantrill's first biographer, called Haller "a young and dauntless spirit" from "an old and wealthy family."[3]

The accuracy of Edwards's description of the Haller family probably depends on one's concept of "old and wealthy," but the scant evidence does suggest that Bill Haller's parents were well respected and relatively well-to-do. Jacob and Jane Haller moved with their children from Pennsylvania to Missouri about 1849 and settled at Independence, the Jackson County seat, where Jacob plied his trade as a mason. In 1850, his real estate was valued at $3,000, a comparatively large sum for the time. Jacob died in 1854, leaving Jane to rear nine children alone, although the oldest, George Washington "Wash" Haller, was virtually grown by this time.[4]

By 1860, Wash, younger brother James Albert "Abe," and one sister had left home, and the two youngest children from the previous census had died. But Bill and three siblings, including one born since 1850, were still living with their mother at Independence. The value of Jane's real estate had grown to $8,200, and she also had $1,000 in personal property. She was, indeed, at least somewhat wealthy by 1860 standards.[5]

Bill Haller had been in the bush with Quantrill about seven months before his shenanigans brought other members of his family under suspicion and ultimately caused them to clash with Federal authorities. About July 1, 1862, a man named William Kerr, acting under dubious authority, went into the Jackson County countryside as a Federal spy and was taken prisoner by some of Quantrill's guerrillas. They took him to their camp, where a debate among the fifteen or so bushwhackers arose on whether they should shoot Kerr. Among those present were Bill Haller and his older brother, Wash, even though Wash was not a regular member of Quantrill's band. On this occasion, however, according to Kerr's later story, Wash was one of those arguing for the spy's execution, and he even offered one of the bushwhackers five dollars to shoot Kerr. Wash was convinced that Kerr knew he (Wash) had been in the habit of feeding the guerrillas, but Quantrill decided to spare Kerr until they could determine whether he'd actually informed on Haller. The guerrilla chieftain detailed Bill Haller, the notorious George Todd, and two other bushwhackers to take the prisoner away from camp and set him free. When the detail got close to Independence, the bushwhackers dismounted, and one of the guerrillas guarded Kerr at the point of a gun while the other three, including Haller and Todd, snuck into town on foot. They came back riding three stolen horses and were fired on as they galloped past the Union pickets. Both Haller and Kerr were wounded by the Federal salvo, and Kerr thought he was also struck by one of Haller's bullets as the guerrillas returned fire.[6]

After his release, Kerr reported to Lieutenant Colonel James T. Buel, the Union commander at Independence, but Buel was skeptical at first of the story told by the so-called spy. He questioned Kerr in particular about Wash Haller, because Haller had always "stood very high in the community as a loyal man." Kerr admitted that aside from the threats Haller had made toward him, he'd never known Haller to be guilty of anything other than bringing food to the guerrillas. After checking out Kerr's story, Buel decided that he was on the level, and considering the circumstances, he felt compelled to place Haller under a $2,000 bond to appear at the Union post when summoned. Reporting the incident a few days later to his commanding officer, Buel mentioned in passing

Confederate guerrilla leader William Quantrill, whose lieutenants included William Haller, son of Jane Haller. *Library of Congress.*

that Kerr had been treated by a Union surgeon and was expected to recover from his wounds.[7]

Just a week or so later, on August 11, Buel's post was attacked by a body of Confederate forces, including Quantrill's guerrilla band, resulting in the First Battle of Independence. In a consolidation of forces, Buel was relieved of his command at Independence in late August and replaced by Colonel William R. Penick. On August 29, just a couple of days after Penick assumed command, Bill Haller's bushwhacking activities brought another member of his family into the clutches of Union military justice. A detachment of Penick's men were on the road from Lexington to Independence when they were fired on from the brush at two different times, and one of the soldiers was killed. Based on what happened a few weeks later, Penick concluded that the noted bushwhacker "Captain Bill Haller," as he was referred to in Union records, had probably done the killing. In early October, a detail of soldiers under Colonel Philip Thompson went into the same vicinity where the shooting took place to arrest Sarah Cox on an unknown charge and found her in company with Jane Haller. They were riding in a carriage with another woman, Sarah Sevier, and the vehicle "showed signs" that the three women "had been carrying provisions to the bushwhackers." Furthermore, when Thompson first stopped the carriage, one of the women called to somebody in the brush to aid that person in getting away. Thompson placed all three women under arrest and brought them back to Independence, where they were lodged in jail.[8]

In reporting the situation to Thomas Gantt, provost marshal general at St. Louis, Penick said he intended to hold the women as prisoners at Independence as long as he remained in command there "to keep them from doing any further mischief to our cause. I regard them as dangerous characters." Penick assured Gantt that the women were "in good quarters and well taken care of."[9]

Something must have happened to change Penick's mind about keeping the women at Independence. In early November, Sarah Cox was paroled to Jackson County after giving bond and taking an oath of allegiance, but Jane Haller had to wait a while longer for her release, because she was under investigation as a subversive. On November 21, Jane was banished to Pennsylvania to live with her deceased husband's sister Catharine, who was married to John Hyssong. The order of banishment was issued by Brigadier General Ben Loan, commanding the Central District of Missouri, and signed by Penick, now acting as provost marshal. Mrs. Haller had five days to leave the state. The banishment of women in Missouri was rare at this relatively early stage of the war, but the fact that Jane's son Bill was a noted guerrilla leader and she was a suspected subversive no doubt accounts for her harsher sentence. The exact disposition of Sarah Sevier's case is unknown.[10]

In early June 1863, Hyssong, a newspaper publisher and justice of the peace in Mercersburg, Pennsylvania, petitioned ex-congressman Edward McPherson for his sister-in-law to be allowed to return to Missouri. Hyssong said Jane Haller now realized that she had "committed an error" and was willing to take an oath of allegiance. Hyssong added that Jane and her three children had been living with his family since the previous fall, and he didn't feel he could continue to keep them. Hyssong emphasized that his sister-in-law had behaved well since she'd lived with him and that he thought she would "be a good Union woman hereafter."[11]

McPherson, an ally of President Lincoln, forwarded the request to the War Department, and in late June, the appeal was granted on condition that both Jane and her fifteen-year-old son take the oath. Jane no doubt returned to Missouri very soon thereafter. Her son Bill had been killed in a skirmish in the spring of 1863, but presumably she got back in time to see another son, Abe, before he, too, was killed in action in the late summer of that year. Jane herself died in 1868 and was buried at Woodlawn Cemetery in Independence.[12]

2

Lizzie Powell

A Beautiful and Accomplished Young Rebel Lady

In early 1863, Lizzie Powell was released unconditionally from Union confinement at Hannibal, even though she was still an outspoken and unapologetic Southern sympathizer and had actively worked to undermine the Union cause in Missouri a few months earlier. Had it been a year later, Lizzie would likely have been sentenced to imprisonment for the duration of the war or at least banished. In late 1862 and early 1863, though, Union officials were still reluctant to deal harshly with women. In Lizzie's case, it didn't hurt, either, that she was a beautiful and intelligent young woman whom "half the Union officers [were] in love with."[13]

Born and reared in northeast Missouri, Lizzie was about twenty-two years old when the Civil War broke out. She first ran afoul of Union authorities in mid- to late September 1862, when she and a friend, twenty-nine-year-old Maggie Creath, took a carriage belonging to a citizen in Monroe County, drove to Hannibal, and "brought out under the protection of the Petticoat Flag a quantity of gun caps, some 50,000, and other essentials to the guerrillas." Miss Creath, according to a Union officer, created quite a sensation "dressed in Rebel colors and a brace of pistols ornamenting her taper waist" as she traveled through Monroe County with guerrilla leader Clay Price. Both women, being "young ladies of large talking propensities," were quite influential in persuading young men of the area to support the Rebel cause.[14]

Maggie was arrested on September 26 and paroled to her father's home in Palmyra. Lizzie was arrested three days later at her sister's home near Santa Fe, Monroe County. Unlike most of the Missouri women arrested during the Civil War, whose stories we know primarily from Union sources, Lizzie kept a diary during her confinement, and it survives. The entry she made at the time of her arrest, like the rest of the diary, clearly shows her plucky, rebellious spirit. The officer in charge of the Union detail that arrested her offered to introduce her to some other officers accompanying the party, but Lizzie demurred, declaring it was not her desire "to be introduced to those whose acquaintance [she] had not sought and did not expect to cultivate."[15]

Taken to the headquarters of Missouri State Militia colonel Edwin Smart, Lizzie was informed that she was being arrested for "discouraging enlistment," urging her friends to fight against the Union, and a number of other offenses. The first charge was a reference to a recent order requiring all able-bodied loyal men not already in Federal service to enlist in the Enrolled Missouri Militia and all Confederate sympathizers to register as disloyal.[16]

Lizzie was held overnight at a nearby residence, where, when quizzed by Union soldiers, she replied with "the most bitter sarcasm" her "excited brain could suggest." The next day, she was taken to Mexico, Missouri, and held there for two days. She was then transported to Hudson City (i.e., Macon), headquarters of Brigadier General Lewis Merrill, who had recently had ten men executed for violating their oaths. Lizzie was taken before General Merrill, whom she called "a cold-blooded fiend." Merrill complimented her as "an intelligent southern lady," and the two talked for almost an hour. They differed greatly in some of their opinions, and at times the discussion turned into "quite a firing of grapeshot and shell in the form of words."[17]

On October 3, Lizzie was taken to Palmyra and held at the National Hotel. On October 4, Provost Marshal William Strachan sent her as a prisoner to the home of Jacob Creath, where she joined her friend Maggie, Jacob's daughter. A few days later, official charges of violating the laws of war and other offenses were drawn up against Lizzie and Maggie with a recommendation that they be banished from Missouri.[18]

Lizzie and Maggie passed their time talking to each other, playing chess, and engaging in other diversions. Lizzie's confinement was starting to depress her, and the gloomy weather the first week of October dampened her spirits even more. Still, she remained defiant toward her Union captors, referring to them as "vile tyrants who infest our state."[19]

On October 8, Colonel Strachan officially informed Lizzie that she was to be banished. Two days later, Lizzie wrote a letter to General Merrill. She felt that she'd been treated courteously while under his guard, and apparently the two had gained a measure of respect for each other despite their heated discussion. Lizzie appealed to the general's sense of charity and his honor as

Left: Lizzie Powell at the time of her imprisonment. *Historical Society of Missouri, Columbia.*

Right: Lizzie Powell was taken before General Lewis Merrill when she was first arrested. *Library of Congress.*

a gentleman to delay or revoke the order of banishment and allow her and Maggie to remain on parole in Missouri.[20]

On October 17, Lizzie received Merrill's answer to her letter, telling her that he would not interfere in her banishment. Lizzie told her diary that she was not disappointed, since it was what she expected. Later the same day, Lizzie learned that ten Rebel prisoners were to be executed in Palmyra the next day by order of General John McNeil in reprisal for the kidnapping and presumed murder of a Union citizen by some partisans under Confederate colonel Joseph Porter, who had recently been recruiting and carrying on an irregular warfare in northeast Missouri. Lizzie and Maggie could only sob and "kneel and pour forth [their] burdened hearts in prayer."[21]

The next morning, Jacob Creath went to General McNeil to plead for mercy for the condemned men, but to no avail. He came back and reported, according to Lizzie, that the general was "lost to all feeling and almost unconsciounably drunk." The executions were carried out as scheduled on the afternoon of October 18. Lizzie was shaken by what she called the "foul deed," which had "plunged not only the city but the whole country in despair and gloom."[22]

Maggie's health began to fail in late October, and she and Lizzie resolved to make a plan of escape if they could not effect their release through legal means. On November 14, Lizzie swallowed her pride and went to General McNeil's headquarters, accompanied by Mr. Creath, to demand an immediate trial. He denied the request but did grant her and Maggie a one-week parole to go to Hannibal.[23]

On November 30, Lizzie again wrote to General Merrill, saying that, despite the unkind manner in which he'd responded to her previous letter, she had decided to write a second time to make one simple inquiry—whether she was to be detained "in this gloomy prison" until her health completely failed. She suggested that he might give her "a more desirable method of ending [her] troublesome existence" by shooting her, since that seemed to be the preferred way of disposing of prisoners in Northeast Missouri. His answer hinged on the question of whether she would have to "assume...the prerogative of liberating [herself]."[24]

Although Lizzie Powell detested General John McNeil for his "butchery" at Palmyra, she swallowed her pride and met with him to try to negotiate her release. *Library of Congress.*

The next day, Maggie Creath called on Colonel Strachan to likewise plead for her and Lizzie's freedom, and Maggie reported back that the young women could only be set free if they would repent and take an oath to the Union. Lizzie immediately shot off a "pithy little note" to Strachan declaring that, since he was interested in her state of mind, she took pleasure in informing him that her conscience was clear in saying that she remained loyal "to the best and most superior man that ever graced a presidential chair" (a reference to Confederate president Jefferson Davis). She added that she would repent when the Federal government repented of its "murderous proceedings and wholesale robberies, its cruelties against the ladies of our once-noble land." Not until then would she "cease to rebel against such petty tyranny."[25]

On December 10, Lizzie, accompanied by Mrs. Creath, again went to see General McNeil, pleading that she was in failing health and that Maggie was even frailer. He again offered to release her upon taking an oath, but she stubbornly refused "to perjure [herself] before God and man." Nevertheless, McNeil granted her a leave of absence to return home until her health was restored.[26]

Although Lizzie was unsatisfied with General Merrill's reply to her first letter, he was apparently moved by her second letter enough to take a personal interest in her case. On December 12, Merrill sent a dispatch to General McNeil asking for a complete report on the cause of Maggie's and Lizzie's arrests and the manner of their confinement. McNeil forwarded the request to Colonel Strachan, who replied on December 13 recounting the young women's September carriage drive from Monroe County to Hannibal carrying gun caps to the guerrillas. Strachan said the women had been paroled to the home of Jacob Creath without a guard until Lizzie had recently been allowed to return to her hometown of Hannibal by McNeil's order. McNeil forwarded Strachen's report to Merrill with a recommendation that the young women be banished or at least closely watched. McNeil said Maggie and Lizzie were notoriously disloyal and "their beauty, talents and superior education have made many a man a bushwhacker."[27]

On December 19, Merrill replied to Lizzie's letter of November 30. He said that, considering the offense she and Maggie were guilty of, he thought they had been treated very leniently and, if it weren't for their sex, would have received much more severe punishment. He told Lizzie her choices were to be banished to a free state such as Indiana or to remain on parole under close surveillance in Missouri. If she chose the former alternative, Merrill would issue an order to that effect.[28]

Lizzie received General Merrill's letter on December 26, but on the same day she also received word from Colonel Strachan that she was released from her parole altogether. Maggie was likewise released unconditionally the same day.[29]

Undeterred by her recent ordeal, Lizzie promptly went back to spreading disloyalty. On January 8, 1863, Hannibal resident William Newland, a Methodist minister, wrote to General Samuel R. Curtis, commanding the Department of the Missouri, complaining that Lizzie, only recently freed from parole, was once again walking the streets of the town "discouraging enlistments," telling her friends to join the Rebel army, and otherwise damaging the Union cause. Since her release, she had made two secretive trips to St. Louis, and she attended parties given in her honor by Southern sympathizers "dressed in rebel colors." Federal officers in Hannibal had been informed of Lizzie's activities, but "about half of them are in love with her." Newland thought Lizzie should be banished or at least taken to St. Louis.[30]

Authorities in St. Louis definitely didn't want Lizzie sent there, because there were already "too many of that kind here." So, General Curtis directed that she be banished, and General Merrill issued an order to that effect on January 12. Lizzie was re-arrested, but she refused the order of banishment and was paroled to her sister's home in Hannibal until officials could determine what to do with her. T.D. Price, assistant provost marshal at Hannibal, wrote to St. Louis on January 20 asking for clarification on what action he should take. Price said that Lizzie, although "quite fascinating," was absolutely incorrigible, and he thought she should be sent south. In the meantime, Price confined Lizzie to a room at the Continental Hotel under guard.[31]

On January 25, Lizzie was taken to a cheaper hotel in Hannibal, after which her health began to deteriorate. Meanwhile, her influential friends began negotiating to have her punishment reduced or revoked. On February 4, Provost Marshal Price wrote to St. Louis authorities again, urging that some definite action be taken in Lizzie's case. Although she had behaved in a "commendable manner" lately, she remained committed to the Southern cause and adamantly refused to obey the order of banishment. Price said he could not continue to keep her imprisoned at Hannibal indefinitely, as no adequate quarters were available. He had even had to defray some of the costs of her confinement out of his own pocket.[32]

On February 25, Price, who himself seemed struck on Lizzie, wrote to Brigadier General T.J. McKean, recommending that she be released unconditionally, mainly because of her declining health. Price said she remained an unrepentant Rebel but that she had behaved well recently and he thought her honor and "pecuniary reasons" would prompt her to be less active in harming the Union cause in the future. McKean, who had recently assumed command of the District of Northeast Missouri, issued an order releasing Lizzie that very day.[33]

On April 27, 1863, Lizzie left Hannibal for the state of Nevada, where she met Alfred Hereford, a young lawyer, and they married in March 1864. The couple lived briefly in St. Joseph, Missouri, before settling in Colorado. They had three children, two of whom survived to adulthood. On August 31, 1877, Lizzie was riding in a carriage with the wife of Colorado governor John Routt when the horses ran away, and Lizzie was thrown from the vehicle. Although a report at the time said she was only slightly injured, she died from complications a little over two months later and was buried in Denver's Riverside Cemetery.[34]

3

Augusta and Zaidee Bagwill

Real Good Rebels

James H. Bagwill of Macon County, Missouri, was the first member of his family to clash with Union authorities during the Civil War. He was arrested and sent to prison in St. Louis in the summer of 1862 for his disloyal activities. Early in the war, he had flown the first Rebel flag in Macon from his house and had put up the second one on a corner near a store he ran. Later, he allegedly shot and mortally wounded a Union soldier. Despite the serious accusations against James Bagwill, his wife and daughter ended up, before the war was over, getting into deeper trouble than he did.[35]

James Bagwill married Jane Hutcheson in Macon County in 1841, and the couple's daughter, Alzada "Zaidee," was born about 1844. Jane died or the couple separated not long afterward, and James married Augusta (maiden name unknown) about 1849. Bagwill was a merchant at Hudson, or Macon, as it was later renamed. After the Civil War broke out, he incurred the wrath of the Union citizens of Macon because of his belligerent disloyalty. Accused of murder and other offenses in August 1862, Bagwill was sent to Gratiot Street Prison, a large building in St. Louis at the corner of Eighth and Gratiot that had been a medical college before the war. He was paroled after just a few weeks. His wife and daughter joined him in St. Louis, and the family took up residence there rather than return to Macon.[36]

Bagwill's brush with Union military authority might have served as a cautionary experience for him, but not for his wife and daughter. Just a few months later, Augusta and Zaidee were arrested after a number of letters to and from Confederate soldiers were intercepted aboard the steamboat *White*

Cloud in early 1863, with at least a couple of the letters bearing Augusta's and Zaidee's names.[37]

Examined on March 26, 1863, Augusta was shown the confiscated letters, marked as Exhibits "A" through "H," and she was asked what she knew about each letter. She admitted she'd written Exhibit "A," a letter dated March 19 and addressed to J.M. Flanigan, an adjutant in the Second Missouri Infantry of Price's army. Much of the letter conveyed everyday news about mutual acquaintances, but toward the end of the missive, Augusta's Rebel sympathies emerged. Among her more incriminating statements was a reference to the Federals occupying Missouri as "Yankee vandals" who "infest our country" and perpetrate "falsehoods and scandals…on an innocent people." Although she would not deign to ask a favor of any Union soldier ranked below colonel, she told Flanigan she could usually get her way with the high-ranking officers by flattering them. However, she said she'd suffered too much at the hands of the Federals to ever forgive them.[38]

Augusta claimed to know nothing about most of the other letters or simply declined to answer questions about them. However, letters "C," "D," and "E" had been bundled together, and she admitted she had written an attached note giving instructions on how to deliver replies to her. This virtual admission that she was acting as an agent for Confederate mail, of course, was at least as damning as any information she might have provided about the letters themselves.[39]

Augusta's nineteen-year-old stepdaughter was also interviewed on March 26. Like Augusta, Zaidee was shown a number of letters marked as alphabetized exhibits. She admitted writing Exhibit "A," a letter from St. Louis dated February 3, 1863, and addressed to W.F. Luckett, who was a soldier in the same Confederate regiment as Flanigan. Beginning the letter "Dear (Darling) Frank," Zaidee told Luckett she feared her letter would not reach him because its carrier was being so closely watched by the Union. Zaidee added that even her own family had to watch what they said, because "Miss Lucy, our 'intelligent contraband,'" might overhear and report the conversation to Union authorities. (This was a reference to the family's Black servant.)[40]

Zaidee said she'd recently gotten a letter from Luckett's mother and that another young woman had said to her (Zaidee) at the time that Mrs. Luckett might let her love Frank if she was "a real good Rebel." Zaidee told Luckett, "If that's all she asks of me, I think you are my property."

Later in the letter, Zaidee vented her Southern sentiments in even stronger language. She confirmed that her father had shot a Union soldier. Bagwill was arrested, and the townspeople of Macon turned against the whole family. In response to threats that their house would be burned, Zaidee and her stepmother moved their belongings to a neighbor's house and then returned to their home and slept on the floor to dissuade the arsonists. When the soldier died six days after Bagwill shot him, "Four great black-hearted villains came bolting into Ma's room and damned us to everything they could, and not a soul in the house but her and I." Finally, in order to survive, Augusta allowed some Union officers to board at the house, but Zaidee refused to socialize with "the contemptible hounds."

"May God speed General Price and his noble army into Missouri," continued Zaidee's letter to her beau, "so that we poor persecuted she-devils (as that elegant paper, the *Republican*, chooses to term us) may have the satisfaction of trampling a few of the negro-loving ladies under our feet." Continuing her racist rant, Zaidee complained of a young lady friend of Luckett's who had recently been attending church with "an American of African descent." She enclosed a notice of an interracial marriage (which she had presumably clipped from a newspaper) as "a specimen of the negro equality that is practiced here among the negro-loving people. I hope to see the last one of them driven into Africa where they can all live together and enjoy their selves in each other's society."

Zaidee told Luckett she'd recently learned that noted Confederate mail runner Absalom Grimes was his cousin, which made her "think a great deal more" of Grimes. Near the end of her letter, Zaidee told her sweetheart to give her love to all the Rebels. "I hope you will give the Feds your best minie balls and shoot a few extra balls in revenge for us." She signed the letter, "Your true and devoted Rebel, Zaidee J. Bagwill."[41]

Except for the one letter she admitted writing, Zaidee, like her stepmother, had little to say about the other letters that were shown to her during her interrogation. She either claimed to know nothing about them or declined to answer questions about them. At one point during the interview, she was asked about Margaret McLure, a St. Louis widow who'd been arrested on March 20 for distributing Rebel mail. McLure's home on Chestnut Street had been confiscated and turned into a female prison. Zaidee said she knew the woman only by sight. She had seen McLure on the street, but McLure had never been to the Bagwill home.[42]

After Zaidee's and Augusta's examinations, they were both ordered to be tried by military commission. Zaidee was charged with corresponding with the enemy and encouraging rebellion against the U.S. government while enjoying its protection. Both charges carried the same two specifications:

Margaret McLure, pictured here in old age, was a Confederate sympathizer who had her St. Louis home confiscated and turned into a women's prison during the Civil War. *Missouri Historical Society, St. Louis.*

that she "did write and attempt to send" a letter to W.F. Luckett, a rebel in arms against the United States, "encouraging the said Luckett and his fellow insurgents" in their rebellion, and that she also attempted to send Luckett a photograph and a pair of gauntlets. Augusta was charged with violating the laws of war and encouraging rebellion against the U.S. government while enjoying its protection. Again, both charges carried the same two specifications: that she attempted to send a letter to an enemy soldier and that she acted as an agent to pass and receive Rebel mail. In support of the first specification, authorities submitted her letter to Flanigan as evidence. To support the second specification, they submitted the letters marked "B," "C," "D," and "E," at least one of which was addressed to parties in the interior of Missouri, and also a bundle of twenty-three letters that were directed to soldiers in the Confederate army.[43]

Zaidee pleaded not guilty to all charges, and her trial began on April 9. Her stepmother and her father were both called as prosecution witnesses, but, not surprisingly, they were uncooperative. For instance, Augusta claimed not to be able to recognize her stepdaughter's handwriting. James said he thought he could recognize Zaidee's handwriting, but when shown Exhibit "A" (the letter to Luckett), he said he could not say for sure it was his daughter's writing. The defense argued that General Orders No. 12, the authority under which Zaidee was tried, did not apply in her case. The order had been issued on February 7, 1863, by General Curtis, and it specified that persons "carrying on treasonable correspondence with the enemy" and rendering the Rebels aid and comfort, whether the persons were "male or female, old or young," were subject to trial by military commission. Zaidee's counsel demanded to know how merely attempting to send letters could be construed as carrying on correspondence with the enemy or lending aid and comfort. In addition, the defense argued that her letter was written before the issuance of General Orders No. 12, that she should have been advised of her right not to answer questions before being interrogated, and that the law was not meant to punish the "innocent though thoughtless correspondence" of a lovestruck girl.[44]

Despite the pleas of the defense, Zaidee was found guilty on all counts. She was sentenced to confinement at home under her oath and a bond of $1,000 to remain there for the duration of the war and not to give aid and comfort to the enemy. Augusta's trial began on April 11, the day after Zaidee's ended, and she, too, pleaded not guilty. Zaidee was called as a witness against her stepmother, but just as Augusta had done in Zaidee's case, the young woman offered little help, saying, for example, that she'd never before seen the letter her stepmother had allegedly written to Flanigan. The arguments in Augusta's case were similar to those presented at Zaidee's trial, and, like her stepdaughter, Augusta was found guilty on all counts. She was sentenced to banishment to the South. The sentences in both cases were promulgated on May 18, but they were mitigated two days later at James Bagwill's request. Instead of going to Dixie, his wife was allowed to go to Canada under $10,000 bond not to give aid and comfort to the enemy, and Zaidee was allowed to accompany her under $5,000 bond. Because of Augusta's ill health, imposition of the sentences was delayed, allowing the women to stay in St. Louis under parole and bond. The sentences were again mitigated in mid-June to allow the mother and stepdaughter to be paroled to Macon County. They were still under bond and a pledge not to give aid and comfort to the enemy, and they were required to report weekly by letter to the provost marshal general's office.[45]

In August, the sentences were once again modified to allow Augusta and Zaidee to come back to St. Louis and take up residence at the Olive Street Hotel, which James Bagwill had acquired in partnership with another man. The family stayed in St. Louis until after the war. Zaidee's sweetheart, William F. Luckett, was mortally wounded in May 1863, and she ended up marrying W.T. Cowan in St. Louis on September 20, 1865. What happened to her after that has not been traced, but her parents later moved to Kansas City, where Bagwill again kept a hotel. The couple next moved to Buchanan County, and after Bagwill died in 1876, Augusta remarried. She died in 1902 and was buried in Mount Mora Cemetery in St. Joseph.[46]

4

Addie Haynes

One of St. Louis's Most Presumptuous Rebels

When Union authorities arrested thirty-year-old Ada "Addie" Haynes in St. Louis on April 1, 1863, they suspected her of a number of disloyal activities and considered her an inveterate Rebel, but about the only thing they could prove against her was that she had written letters to her brothers serving in the Confederate army. She admitted as much when they interviewed her later the same day. Her examiner also thought she was insolent, because she balked at answering some of his questions. That was enough to get her banished to Dixie.[47]

Born in Ireland in 1834, Addie Howard came to the United States with her family in 1847 and settled in St. Louis. She married Christopher Haynes when she was just fourteen or fifteen years old, and by 1855, the couple had three children. Addie's husband died about the time the youngest child was born, leaving her to support three kids. In the late 1850s, she taught in the boys department of the South Freeman School in St. Louis. In 1858, she temporarily lost her job for unknown reasons but was reinstated by the St. Louis School Board on a 10–3 vote.[48]

Addie started corresponding with Confederate soldiers and aiding Rebel prisoners held in St. Louis–area prisons at least as early as the spring of 1862, but it was a year later before Union officials gathered enough intelligence to arrest her on suspicion of carrying and receiving Rebel mail. During her interview on April 1, 1863, she was asked about Confederate mail runner Absalom Grimes. Addie admitted she'd heard of him but denied being acquainted with him. Had Grimes ever carried letters to her from her friends in the South? "Not that I know of," Addie replied.[49]

Asked about a couple of other men suspected of involvement in delivering or receiving Confederate mail, she admitted that she was acquainted with them but denied having ever aided them in any clandestine mail operation.[50]

It was when Addie was asked about her own family that she got snippy, and her defiance likely got her into as much trouble as her alleged disloyal activities. When asked whether she had any relations in the Rebel army, she first told her examiner she didn't consider herself obliged to answer the question. Later, she relented and admitted she had two brothers in the Confederate army, but she didn't know where in the South they were at the time. She said she'd sent a number of letters to them with instructions that the letters be destroyed if her brothers could not be located, but she would not disclose by whom she had sent them. She had never received any letters from her brothers, Addie said, but her mother had. Pressed on exactly how many times she had written to her brothers, Addie said, "I decline to answer." But she again relented and said she hadn't kept count and didn't know how many. By whom, her examiner insisted, did Addie send the last letter she wrote to her brothers? "I could not tell," she declared, "and even if I did remember, I would not tell you."[51]

Addie's testy refusal to answer the examiner's questions probably sealed her fate. Assistant Provost Marshal General R.M. Swander forwarded the transcript of the examination to his superior with a recommendation that Addie be "sent beyond the lines of the U.S. forces." Since the beginning of the war, Swander declared, she had been "one of the most notorious rebels and agent for carrying the mail to the rebels." She was also "one of the most insolent and presumptuous rebels St. Louis has."[52]

It's not clear whether Addie was imprisoned when she was first arrested, but at some point in April or early May she was confined at the Chestnut Street Female Military Prison, Mrs. McLure's former home.[53]

On May 13, Addie, Mrs. McLure, and nine other women were banished to the South under orders from General Curtis. They were the first women

FIRST INSTALLMENT OF THE BANISHED.

Thirteen Men and Ten Women Dispatched for Vicksburg.

SOME 200 MORE TO GO.

A headline in a St. Louis newspaper announces the first Civil War banishment of Missouri citizens to the South. Addie Haynes was among the initial group of exiles. *From the* St. Louis Daily Missouri Democrat.

sent to Dixie from St. Louis during the Civil War. Union authorities had previously been reluctant to be seen as "making war on women"; however, the Lieber Code, issued by President Lincoln less than a month before to codify the U.S. laws of war, specified, among many other things, that "the law of war, like the criminal law regarding other offenses, makes no difference on account of the difference of sexes, concerning the spy, the war-traitor, or the war-rebel."[54]

The exiles were taken down the Mississippi River by steamboat to Memphis. From there, Addie made her way to Okolona, Mississippi, and then to Columbus, Mississippi. Later, she made a trip to Mobile, Alabama, and stopped briefly at Meridian, Mississippi, on the return trip, but she spent most of her banishment at Columbus.[55]

General Samuel R. Curtis, who issued the order banishing Addie Haynes. *Library of Congress.*

Addie had taken her eleven-year-old son with her, but she'd been forced to leave her nine-year-old son with her mother. Her fifteen-year-old daughter was left in the care of an orphanage. She heard from her family only once, according to her later story, and that was indirectly through a third party. She learned at the time that her children were suffering and in need of her care. She wrote two letters seeking permission to return to St. Louis to see to her children's care but received no answers. In late March 1864, she decided to return on her own authority. She had $500 in Confederate money when she started the trip but exchanged it for government currency before coming within the Federal lines at Memphis on March 25. At Memphis, without reporting herself as an exile, she obtained a pass to Cairo, Illinois. There she boarded a boat bound for St. Louis and was never asked for a pass.[56]

Addie reached St. Louis on the evening of the twenty-eighth, spent the night with her mother, and reported to the provost marshal's office the next morning, seeking permission to stay in St. Louis. Instead, she was immediately lodged in the St. Charles Street Female Prison for violation of her banishment order. Examined on April 1, exactly one year after her first interrogation, she recited the story of her banishment and said she wasn't even sure why she'd been sent south to begin with, although she'd heard something about a charge of being a Rebel mail agent. Addie assured her examiner she'd brought no written or verbal communications with her when she returned and that she'd only come back out of concern for her children's welfare.[57]

Addie said she still felt concern and empathy for her brothers in the Confederate army but beyond their safety and welfare cared nothing for the South or those who engaged in the rebellion. She desired to be released on taking an oath and would "religiously adhere to and respect her obligations" if her request was granted. She stated, however, perhaps as a way of suggesting where her first loyalty lay, that she was born in Ireland and had never renounced her allegiance to Great Britain.[58]

On April 13, Addie wrote a letter to an unidentified St. Louis citizen seeking his help in getting her released. She said she thought her children were suffering, and she added also that she was in need of clothes. Prison officials intercepted the letter and turned it over to the provost marshal general's office. From its fairly innocuous content, it's not clear why the letter was considered contraband, except that it was probably frowned upon for prisoners to implore others to intercede on their behalf. At any rate, a different citizen did intervene on Addie's behalf while she was at St. Charles Street Prison. Josiah Fogg wrote an undated letter to Provost Marshal General John Sanderson pleading that Mrs. Haynes was "a poor helpless widow" who'd lost her husband several years earlier and had since struggled to support her kids. Fogg thought that, when Addie had gotten into trouble the previous year for disloyal activities, wealthy, influential citizens had made a tool of her by enticing her to say and do things that she never would have done on her own, while her instigators "were enjoying the comforts of home and the protection of your department." Fogg considered Mrs. Haynes "entirely harmless" on her own and not inclined to damage the Union cause unless persuaded by others to do mischief.[59]

Fogg's letter failed to sway Union authorities, and Addie remained in custody. So, the fate she suffered three months later must have been based solely on her speech and behavior while confined at the female prison. On July 9, Colonel Sanderson wrote to General William Rosecrans, commander of the Department of the Missouri, recommending the banishment of four women. The first three he thought should be sent south, but Addie Haynes was a special case. He thought sending her to Dixie would only be accommodating her. She'd come into Federal lines in violation of orders, and she had already "accomplished probably all she came for." (Sanderson did not make clear when and how he thought Addie had accomplished the disloyal purpose of her mission.) If the statement Addie gave shortly after her return could safely be relied on, Sanderson noted, she would be entitled to leniency. However, "her whole demeanor since her arrival, in every way, directly and emphatically contradicts the sincerity and truthfulness of her statement."[60]

In keeping with Sanderson's recommendation, General Rosecrans issued an order on July 20 requiring Addie to take an oath, give bond, and be banished to New York. During her exile, she came under suspicion of aiding a Confederate conspiracy to burn New York City, and Union authorities confined her to a room at the Metropolitan Hotel for ten days before she was cleared of the charge. In mid-January 1865, Addie's mother, Catherine Howard, wrote to Colonel James H. Baker, who had taken over as provost marshal general of the Department of the Missouri, imploring him to allow Addie to come back to St. Louis. Mrs. Howard said she had requested that Addie come back home the previous year, not realizing her daughter might be arrested for it. Mrs. Howard said there were other women who'd returned from banishment and not been molested. She concluded that, if Colonel Baker would permit her daughter to return to her children in St. Louis, she was sure Addie would "conduct herself in the future with perfect loyalty."[61]

Mrs. Howard's request was granted, and Colonel Baker wrote a letter to Addie in New York notifying her of the terms under which she could return. Addie wrote back on March 10, 1865, saying that she gladly accepted the kind offer and assuring Baker that she would fulfill the conditions of her return.[62]

Addie came back to St. Louis and lived there the rest of her long life. She never remarried, and her children continued to live with her until they were old themselves. Addie's Rebel spirit was still apparent when she gave an interview about 1915 at the age of eighty-one. Speaking of the unsuccessful plot to burn New York, she offered as her defense an assertion that, if she'd been involved, "*she* would have done a better job." Addie died in 1924 at the age of ninety, and she was buried at St. Matthew Cemetery in St. Louis.[63]

5

Lucie Nicholson

The Belle of Boonville

Unlike many Missouri women who were arrested by Union authorities during the Civil War, Lucie Nicholson of Cooper County had no close relatives in the Southern army. Yet probably no woman in the state was more active or outspoken in her support of the Confederate cause than Lucie. She seems to have been motivated by deeply held conviction and not so much by relational ties as were many of the women arrested only for feeding and harboring guerrillas. But even Lucie had an interest in the war beyond her devotion to principle. Although none of her close relatives were Southern soldiers, she was engaged to one.

Born on July 10, 1827, in Maryland, Lucie came to Missouri with her siblings and parents, William and Mary Nicholson, in the mid-1830s and settled in Cooper County a few miles south of Boonville. Her parents came from "old Southern stock" and were among the prominent slaveholders of Cooper County. As a young woman, Lucie was known as "the belle of Boonville" and was considered "a mighty pretty girl." Shortly before the Civil War, she became engaged to David Herndon Lindsay, a recent widower and principal of the Saline Female Institute in Miami, Missouri, but the couple decided to postpone the wedding because of "the distracted condition of the country."[64]

From the very beginning of the war, Lucie was active in support of the Southern cause. After Governor Jackson's and General Price's Missouri State Guard forces were routed by General Lyon at the Battle of Boonville on June 17, 1861, she set up a field hospital near her hometown and tended to the needs of the wounded Southern soldiers until the last one was able to be moved. Writing from Cooper County a week after the battle, another local woman, Nancy Chapman Jones, dubbed Lucie "the Florence Nightingale of Boonville." Days after the fight at Boonville, David Lindsay, Lucie's fiancé, joined Price's army at Lexington and was later commissioned a major.[65]

In the fall of 1861, thirty-three-year-old Lucie traveled to Osceola to rendezvous with Price, bringing morphine and other drugs. She then accompanied his army to Springfield, where she and other young women sewed clothing for the soldiers. According to Lucie, Price even swore her into regular military service and promised her a commission. After Price abandoned Springfield at the approach of Federal forces in early 1862, Lucie headed back to Cooper County. She was arrested once she reached home, local authorities having learned of her trip to Springfield. She was taken to Boonville and held prisoner there for eight weeks by Lieutenant Colonel Joseph Eppstein, commanding the post. Lieutenant Colonel Thomas T. Crittenden ordered her release in the spring of 1862.[66]

Thomas T. Crittenden, shown here several years after the war, ordered Lucie Nicholson released from confinement at Boonville in early 1862. *Library of Congress.*

After her release, Lucie taught school near Rocheport in Boone County. She was still there when she wrote a letter to her sister Gettie (Gertrude) on April 25, 1863, which would land her in a heap of trouble. She told Gettie that Federal authorities in Boone and neighboring counties were stirred up by the presence in the region of Sidney Jackman, a Confederate colonel who'd come into his home territory of north Missouri to gather recruits but who was waging guerrilla warfare in the meantime. Lucie said Union general Odon Guitar had threatened to burn Jackman's brother's house and their uncle's house if Jackman did not leave the area. Lucie thought, if Guitar carried out his threat, at least four Union houses would be burned in retaliation.[67]

And she was just getting warmed up in giving vent to her Southern sympathies. "Oh, how I wish Price would come," Lucie told her sister. "I would rather see every house in Mo. burned to the ground than see it remain in the power of the Fed. gov." Later she told Gettie that she thought she had been of considerable service to the Confederate cause, and "come weal or woe," she intended to keep doing it. Lucie assured Gettie that she was not putting their mother in danger, because their mother couldn't be held responsible for the acts of a daughter who was over twenty-one. She was being very careful, Lucie continued, because she did "not care to be banished to Dixie, dearly as I love the cause."[68]

Lucie said she was devoted to General Price and had also "struck up a little correspondence" with Colonel Jackman. She ended her letter by saying that, despite her strong Rebel sympathies, "I do wish we could have peace. The horrid carnage that now deluges the land makes my heart ache."[69]

Lucie may have assured her sister that she was being very careful, but almost immediately after writing the letter, she made a terrible blunder. Very near the time she wrote her letter to Gettie, she also wrote to James Wilhite, a Boone County resident held prisoner at Gratiot Street Prison in St. Louis, and she inadvertently placed each letter in the wrong envelope. Gettie's letter, mailed to Wilhite, was intercepted by Union authorities in St. Louis, and on April 28, Colonel Franklin. A. Dick, provost marshal general of the Department of the Missouri, ordered Lucie's arrest. She was taken into custody on May 3 and sent to St. Louis, where she was lodged in the Gratiot Street Prison. She was put in the same room with Mrs. Mary Louden, who'd been arrested about a week earlier for smuggling Rebel mail. (Mary's husband, Robert Louden, was a partner of noted Confederate mail runner Absalom Grimes.) Years after the war, Lucie remembered jailkeeper William Masterson as "a horrid man" who mistreated her and especially Mrs. Louden. Lucie was also repulsed by the food and sanitary conditions in the hospital. Whenever workers cleaned the prison hospital, water would pour down on the women in their room directly below the hospital.[70]

Charged with being "a volunteer in the rebel army," Lucie was interrogated on May 5. She readily admitted that she had written the letter in question, and she explained how she had gotten it and the letter to Wilhite mixed up. Yes, she knew Wilhite but was not related to him. She had gone to Price's army to do whatever she could for the Southern cause, and she had since written letters to General Price and had received letters from other Confederate officers. She said her mother did not know about her going to Springfield in the fall of 1861 and did not approve of it when she found out. Lucie herself, on the other hand, was "Southern heart and soul" and "would like very much to see the Confederacy established and then live under Jeff

Davis." In fact, she supposed her whole purpose was "being a Southern woman." If so, she added, "I am steeped in it mighty deep."[71]

She frequently corresponded with Rebel officers and had recently received a note from Colonel Jackman suggesting that Price's army would soon reenter Missouri. She told her examiner she didn't know of anyone else in Boone County who wrote letters to Southern soldiers. "If I did know it," she added, "I would not tell you." Yes, she knew a good number of people in St. Louis, but she didn't know of any of them writing letters to the Rebel army either.[72]

On May 8, Lucie and Mrs. Louden were transferred to the Chestnut Street Female Prison. On May 13, they joined Mrs. McLure, Addie Haynes, and seven other women in banishment to the South. Among the other banished women was Lily Frost, wife of Daniel M. Frost, who had been commander of the Missouri militia at Camp Jackson and was now a general in the Confederate army. In addition to the women ordered south, two women whose husbands were exiled at the same time requested and were granted permission to accompany the group. In an article announcing the banishments, the *St. Louis Daily Missouri Republican* reprinted in its entirety the letter Lucie had written to her sister.[73]

Some of the banished women, including Addie Haynes, had children who had to be left behind. Years later, Lucie remembered the heartrending scenes between the children and their mothers as the women prepared to leave. "You never heard such screaming," she recalled. The ladies were taken by carriage to a landing on the Mississippi River, where they boarded the *Belle Memphis*. Many spectators were at the landing to see the banished men and women off, but the leave-taking had mostly taken place earlier.[74]

The women disembarked at Memphis, where they went their separate ways. Lucie was placed in a carriage with Mrs. McLure, Mrs. Frost, and two other ladies, and they were driven to Columbus, Mississippi. On June 23, one of the other banished women sent word to General Price that "his little friend Miss Lucie Nicholson" was at Columbus, but it's not clear whether Lucie was actually still there on that date, because, a few weeks after arriving at Columbus, she left for Arkansas, still in company with Lily Frost.[75]

In Arkansas, Lucie rendezvoused with Major Lindsay, and they were married at Pine Bluff on July 22, 1863, at General Frost's headquarters. Lucie remained in the South throughout the remainder of the war, moving back and forth "pillar to post" with the Confederate army. She spent her time comforting the wounded, raising money to clothe the soldiers, and providing whatever other help she could. She also found time to continue her

Left: Lily Frost was among the women banished at the same time as Lucie Nicholson. *Missouri Historical Society, St. Louis.*

Right: General Sterling Price considered Lucie Nicholson his "little friend." *Library of Congress.*

correspondence with Confederate officers. On August 5, 1863, just a couple of weeks after her marriage to David Lindsay, a soldier in the regiment of Colonel Robert McCulloch, who was camped near Looxahoma, Mississippi, wrote in his diary that the colonel, who was from Lucie's home territory of Cooper County, had recently received a letter from her. Presumably the letter was written before Lucie married Lindsay, since the soldier referred to her as "Miss Nicholson," although he might simply have been unaware of the marriage.[76]

When the war ended, Lucie and her husband went to his native state of Kentucky, and David resumed his career as a schoolmaster and professor. In 1876, the couple returned to Missouri and settled in Clinton County, where David was a prominent citizen for many years. After his death in 1902, Lucie lived with her daughter in Missouri and Oklahoma. About 1912, she gave an interview to a woman who was collecting stories of Missouri women during the Civil War for the Daughters of the Confederacy. After relating some of her wartime experiences, Lucie concluded that she could never forget nor forgive the mistreatment that she thought she and others had endured at the hands of Unionists, but she was willing to go so far as to "wish them no harm."[77]

About 1921, Lucie moved to St. Louis to live with her three sisters. On April 3, 1923, the sisters' house caught fire. One of Lucie's sisters perished in the blaze, and Lucie, now ninety-five, died at a hospital a few hours later from her burns. At the time of her death, a neighbor remarked that Lucie and her sisters had been proud Southern ladies, even in old age, but they were also known as generous to the poor and willing to help anyone in need.[78]

Lucie's body was taken back to Clinton County and buried in the Lathrop Cemetery beside her deceased husband.[79]

6

Hattie Snodgrass

Proud Spirit of a Southern Lady

Another woman banished at the same time as Addie Haynes and Lucie Nicholson was twenty-eight-year-old Harriet "Hattie" Snodgrass of St. Louis. Being banished wasn't the only thing the three women had in common; all three were schoolteachers. Hattie had a couple of other things in common with Lucie. Like Lucie, she had no blood relatives in the Southern army, her closest kin being a brother-in-law. However, Hattie, again like Lucie, was even more outspoken and dedicated in her support of the Confederacy than most of the women of rural Missouri who were arrested primarily for feeding and harboring their loved ones in the bush.

Not only did Hattie have no close kinship ties to the Rebel army, but also neither she nor her parents had Southern roots. Yet, after the Civil War broke out, she became an active agent of the Confederate war effort, risking her freedom and well-being to execute daring assignments like spying and smuggling contraband into the area's military prisons. Indeed, few Missouri women, if any, were more defiant or active in their devotion to the Southern cause than Harriet Snodgrass.[80]

A native of Pennsylvania, Hattie moved with her family to St. Louis when she was a child. In 1850, she lived in the Sixth Ward with her parents, two older sisters, and a younger brother. During the 1850s, she taught at the Seventh Street School between Washington and Franklin avenues with Margaret McLure, but in 1860, she was staying in Callaway County with the Lakenan family. Returning to St. Louis in the early 1860s, she resumed her teaching career and lived with her sister Teresa, who had married Joseph Clayton.[81]

Hattie and the rest of the Clayton household resided at No. 21 Brooklyn Street when Hattie's disloyal activities attracted the scrutiny of her neighbors in early 1863. One or more of the neighbors reported her to Federal authorities about the first of May, and officials began taking depositions against her on May 5. Lewis Vandewater testified that he'd known Hattie for about eleven years and that, ever since the outbreak of the war, she had been "an open and avowed secessionist." Vandewater said he'd heard Hattie hurrah for Jeff Davis and that he'd been told she kept a Secesh flag in her schoolroom. Known secessionists were in the habit of leaving parcels at the Snodgrass residence, and every two or three weeks, usually on a Friday, Hattie would make a trip to the Alton Military Prison in nearby Alton, Illinois, taking the packages with her.[82]

On May 6, Hattie's next-door neighbor Henry Hardaway said he'd been acquainted with Miss Snodgrass for about ten years, she was an avowed secessionist, and her home was "the resort of notorious Rebel sympathizers," including the family of the late John M. Winer. (Winer was a former mayor of St. Louis and a Confederate lieutenant colonel who was killed at the Battle of Hartville in January 1863.) Hardaway said Hattie received packages from Southern sympathizers, which she, in turn, delivered to the Alton prison every alternate Friday or Saturday. He, like Vandewater, said she was known to hurrah for Jeff Davis and to display a Rebel flag. On the previous Monday, Hardaway had seen Hattie, in front of her house in the company of some other ladies, wrap a handkerchief embroidered with red around her neck and proclaim that those were her colors.[83]

The next day, another of Hattie's neighbors, Charles Kauffman, said he'd lived in the Snodgrass neighborhood only about a year but had observed that, although Hattie "was living in apparently humble circumstances, her house was the resort of the wealthy and fashionable secessionists of St. Louis." Kauffman reported that his family had been kept awake for about an hour in the middle of the previous night by the sound of heavy boxes being moved at the Snodgrass residence. Kauffman thought the boxes were being moved in preparation for delivery to the Alton prison.[84]

On Saturday, May 9, Hattie was arrested at her residence and ordered to report to the provost marshal's office in St. Louis, where she was interrogated by Captain Swander about the activities her neighbors had accused her of. Hattie admitted that her sister's husband, Joseph Clayton, was in the Southern army. She wasn't sure whether he was a captain or a major, although she had heard he was a quartermaster. Asked from whom she had heard this, Hattie replied, "I won't answer that question."

"Why?" asked Swander.

"Because I don't wish to answer the question," she repeated stubbornly. She then explained that she did not want to answer any questions about letters she may have written to persons in the Southern army.[85]

When Swander asked whether she had ever received letters to forward to persons in the Southern army, she replied that she had not. Pressed as to whether she had ever kept a Rebel flag in the house in which she lived, she replied, "No, sir, not in the house in which I live."[86]

Hattie admitted wrapping a white handkerchief with crimson embroidery around her neck on Monday evening, as Mr. Hardaway had claimed, but she denied saying then or at any other time that red, white, and red were her colors. She admitted she had hurrahed for Jeff Davis, and she also admitted she had delivered packages to the Alton Military Prison. However, she said that the parcels contained nothing but clothing and other necessary provisions for the prisoners, that she had delivered them to the hospital department of the prison, and that she had always paid her own expenses in traveling to Alton.[87]

Hattie said she was acquainted with Mrs. John W. Winer and had called socially at the Winer home. On the occasion of John Winer's funeral, some members of the provost marshal's office were in attendance, and Hattie admitted making a critical remark about William K. Patrick, one of the Union officers. Specifically, she said she never thought Will Patrick would "stoop so low" as to approach a corpse with his hat on, but she denied calling him a "Lincoln hireling."[88]

When Swander asked how long her brother-in-law had been in the Rebel army, Hattie promptly corrected him. "Confederate, sir, not Rebel army."

After volunteering that Clayton had joined the army the previous July or August, Hattie abruptly ended the interview. "And now, Captain," she announced, "I think I have answered questions enough and will not answer any more. Whatever the government wishes to do with me they can do, but no more questions will I answer." In a final show of defiance, Hattie then refused to sign the deposition.[89]

After the interview, Swander wrote a brief of her case and forwarded it and a transcript of the interview to Colonel Dick, provost marshal general, with a recommendation that she be sent south. At or near the time of Hattie's arrest, a letter she had written on May 7 came into Union hands, and it, too, was added to her file.[90]

The letter was addressed to Lieutenant Colonel J.H. Dougherty of the Confederate army, then being held at Myrtle Street Prison, and it read as follows:

> *I see by the papers that you are again a prisoner of war. I should have written sooner, but I left the city on Friday for Alton and returned this morning. Can you tell me anything of Capt. Clayton? Please send me the names of Burbridge's men that are with you & a list of the clothing they may need & I will endeavor to supply them. Hoping to hear from you soon. My friend sends her kindest regards to you. Your friend, Hattie E. Snodgrass.*

The "Capt. Clayton" Hattie inquired about was, of course, her brother-in-law, while the "Burbridge" to whom she referred was Colonel John Q. Burbridge, commanding the Fourth Missouri Cavalry. Largely recruited at St. Louis, this was the same regiment to which John M. Winer had belonged.[91]

Accused of being a "Rebel mail agent," Hattie Snodgrass was imprisoned at Mrs. McLure's old home on Chestnut Street to await banishment to the South. The banishment order directed that Hattie be taken down the Mississippi River by steamboat to Memphis and then on to Vicksburg or some other suitable point within the lines of the Confederate army, not to return without the permission of the U.S. secretary of war. On May 13, the very day her banishment order was issued, Hattie was sent south with Lucie Nicholson and company. Hattie's sister Teresa Clayton accompanied Hattie at her own request. Others making the trip included Hattie's former colleague Margaret McLure. Colonel Dick, in issuing the order, told Major T.J. McKinney, who was charged with carrying it out, that he should make sure Hattie's luggage was carefully searched and that he should take every care to deliver her and the families accompanying her safely.[92]

Despite Hattie's banishment, Union authorities had not quite heard the last of her. On June 23, 1863, she wrote a letter from Mobile, Alabama, to Colonel Burbridge, who was somewhere in Arkansas. She reminded the colonel of a previous letter she'd written to him prior to being banished in which she provided him an account of the "terrible outrages perpetuated upon the remains of our noble patriots, Col. John M. Winer & Col. [Emmett] MacDonald." Little did she think at the time, Hattie added, that the next time she corresponded with Burbridge she would be in exile "many, many miles from home." She said that the "Yankee thieves" had

A Mississippi River steamboat similar to those that carried the exiled women from St. Louis to Dixie. *Library of Congress.*

thought they would crush her spirit and that of the Southern-sympathizing women who had accompanied her south, but that, upon their departure, none of them had shed a tear or shown any sign of weakness and, instead, had exchanged only cheerful words. The Federals had allowed some of the friends and loved ones of the exiles to come aboard the steamboat preparatory to the departure. Hattie said she thought they had only done so with the expectation of gloating over any exhibition of feeling on the part of the Southerners, but she and her friends did not give them the satisfaction. Didn't the fools know, Hattie asked rhetorically, that the very sight of them would be enough to stifle any emotion? "Oh, I never knew what it was to hate until now," she exclaimed.[93]

Hattie's account of the scene at the St. Louis landing contradicts Lucie Nicholson's recollection years later of an emotional leave-taking, but the heartrending spectacle Lucie remembered may well have taken place before the women reached the boat. The day after the departure, the *St. Louis Daily Missouri Democrat* reported that the goodbyes had mostly been said before the women reached the landing.[94]

After describing the departure, Hattie provided Colonel Burbridge a mocking account of her interview at the provost marshal's office in St. Louis. She told him that, when she was asked whether she had ever had a Rebel flag in her home, she had replied, "No, sir," because she "did not think it worthwhile" to correct the examiner and tell him it was a Confederate flag. Hattie thanked God that the so-called Rebel flag was now waving over the fields of Arkansas, and she yearned for the day when it would be greeted by "the downtrodden and oppressed Missourians. How much longer are our people to be insulted and our prisoners murdered! This inactivity is killing me. Here I am doing nothing, nothing for our cause."[95]

Speaking of herself and her fellow refugees, Hattie said, "We are all anxious to get into Arkansas to our 'natural protectors.'" Moving her and her friends close to their male family members, Hattie explained, was one of the rationales Union officials had offered for sending them south, and now that the banishment had been accomplished, many of them were indeed anxious to reunite with brothers, husbands, or other male acquaintances in Arkansas. Hattie, for one, obviously did not feel she needed protection or that being sent south was any sort of favor.

Colonel John Q. Burbridge, with whom Hattie Snodgrass corresponded. *Missouri Historical Society, St. Louis.*

Hattie said her sister Mrs. Clayton sent her love to Burbridge's wife and that, although she (i.e., Hattie) did not know Burbridge's wife, she sent hers, too. Hattie closed the letter by saying that she hoped the Yankees would soon "be destroyed, annihilated, or anything else that will get them out of the way. I remain, Your friend, Hattie E. Snodgrass."[96]

Colonel Burbridge was captured on August 24, 1863, near Brownsville, Arkansas. Hattie's letter was found among his belongings and later used as evidence against him. He spent about seven months in Union prisons before being exchanged in 1864.[97]

Meanwhile, Hattie slipped back into St. Louis in the summer of 1864, in defiance of the banishment order against her, bringing news and letters from Confederate soldiers to their loved ones in Missouri. Another reason for her visit was to see her aged mother, Jane Snodgrass. However, she intended to return south, and she recruited two other Southern ladies who wished to accompany her.[98]

Hattie adopted an alias, calling herself "Miss Miller," but she was so well known in St. Louis that she still had to delegate certain errands to the other women for fear of being recognized on the streets. Preparatory to the trip, the women packed letters, gold, Confederate gray clothes, and other contraband into trunks or secreted them on their persons. One of the other ladies, Hannah Rainwater, recalled years later that Hattie had so much contraband that a friend advised her not to try to take it all or she would surely be caught. So, she repacked and left one of her trunks behind.[99]

When the women boarded a boat in October for the trip south, a clerk aboard the craft recognized Miss Snodgrass and called her by name, but the captain, who was sympathetic to Hattie's mission, quickly corrected him, saying "You are mistaken. That is Miss Miller." The young man, who had been a Sunday school pupil of Hattie's, promptly adopted the ruse and thereafter referred to her as "Miss Miller."[100]

The women expressed such a carefree willingness to have their luggage searched that the Union detective on board the steamboat conducted only a cursory inspection, and all went well until the party reached Memphis, where they were questioned as to their destination and purpose. Hattie, still going by the surname Miller, told the Union authorities that she was originally from Pennsylvania, had taught school for several years in Arkansas, had been north to attend to business, and was now returning to Arkansas. Hannah, the younger of the other two women, was supposedly a friend who was going to stay with Hattie, while the older woman was a friend of Hattie's mother who was going south for her health. The women were allowed to continue their journey but first were compelled to take an oath of allegiance to the United States.[101]

During the entire trip, Hattie acted as spokesperson and "captain" for the small party of women. At one point during the journey, she got into a spat with a Union detective and impulsively told him, "I am Southern from the crown of my head to the soles of my feet," but the detective, who had provoked the confrontation, let the matter drop.[102]

When the little group finally reached its destination, the women were standing on the deck of the boat getting ready to go ashore, with Hattie conversing with a Union captain, when the captain suddenly asked whether she had any letters. No, just "a verbal message for a lady who went to Texas before the war," Hattie replied calmly, despite the fact that the handbag she was carrying, which was almost touching the captain, "would have told a different story."[103]

Near the end of the war, Hattie traveled to Washington, D.C., where she got her banishment order revoked and was allowed to return to St. Louis. After her mother died post-1880, Hattie moved to Texas and lived near Texarkana with her brother for a number of years, but she eventually returned to St. Louis. She was living on Fairmount Street in 1911 when William Thomas briefly recounted her wartime adventures in his *History of St. Louis County*. Hattie apparently died shortly afterward, having never married and having never forsaken her proud Southern spirit.[104]

7

Marion W. Vail

Confederate Mail Smuggler

About the time Hattie Snodgrass and her companions were steamboating for Dixie in mid-May 1863, another St. Louis woman, Marion W. Vail, clashed with Federal authorities in the city for activities similar to those that had gotten Hattie in trouble just a week or so earlier. Like Hattie, Marion Vail actively supported the Confederate war effort in Missouri despite having no close relatives fighting for the cause.

A native of Kentucky, Marion Owens married New Jersey–born Corra O. Vail in St. Louis on October 25, 1849, when she was nineteen. The couple took up residence in the city's Fifth Ward, and Corra Vail took a job as a clerk. In the early 1850s, Vail went into business for himself, opening a clothing store in partnership with W.F. Kelley. By 1860, Mr. and Mrs. Vail had two children, a nine-year-old son, Owen, and a seven-year-old daughter, Cora.[105]

Marion began her clandestine activities on behalf of the Confederacy at least as early as the spring of 1862. In late March, she visited Confederate soldier Absalom Grimes at Myrtle Street Prison after he had been captured at the Battle of Pea Ridge and transported to St. Louis. Marion saw Grimes, whom she'd known since before the war, again when he escaped a few days after her visit, and she soon became involved in the Confederate mail-running operation that ultimately made him notorious. Marion and other Southern-sympathizing women would gather letters from St. Louis citizens for delivery by Grimes to their loved ones in the Confederate army, and on Grimes's return, they would distribute the letters written by Rebel soldiers to their families in St. Louis that he brought back. When Grimes was recaptured in late September 1862 and held at Gratiot Street Prison in St. Louis, Marion visited him again both before and after his escape from that facility. Marion earned a reputation, in the estimation of at least one Union officer, as "the worst rebel in town," but she did not become the subject of an official investigation until the spring of 1863, when it was alleged that she had harbored Grimes after his prison escape the previous fall and perhaps even aided him in the escapade.[106]

Arrested on or before May 18, Marion was taken to the provost marshal's office for interrogation. She admitted that she had visited Grimes at the Myrtle Street facility during his first imprisonment in the spring of 1862 and had seen him shortly after his escape. However, she denied that she had visited him at Gratiot Street Prison during the fall of 1862. "I did not see him in that prison," she said, "although I tried hard enough, I assure you." Marion claimed that she and her sister Lizzie Pickering were in Warren County visiting another sister, Mrs. Tesson, until a day or two before Grimes escaped and that she knew nothing about the breakout until after the fact, although she suspected that an attempt might be made. She also denied any involvement in distributing Rebel letters that Lizzie's husband, John Pickering, was alleged to have recently brought from the South.[107]

Marion admitted that she saw Grimes after his escape from Gratiot and that he told her how the feat was accomplished, but she declined to reveal at whose house she saw him. Grimes went south shortly after his escape, and Marion said she received a letter from him about a month later. She also said she had heard indirectly from Grimes about six weeks ago through a man who had seen him in Mississippi but that she had not received any letters from the South in over two months.[108]

Marion acknowledged that, in addition to Grimes, she was also acquainted with Colonel B.F. Parker and that she had received a letter from him ten days prior to her interrogation. It was written at Yellville, Arkansas, and mailed at Pleasant Hope, Missouri. Marion said Parker, who'd been a prisoner in St. Louis the previous spring and summer, did not expect an answer to his letter. Knowing she might be concerned about his well-being, he had merely written to her to let her know he was all right. She emphasized that Parker was not a relative of hers and that she had no relatives in the Confederate army. She said she had not written to him since he was in prison. Marion later added that Grimes and Parker were her only friends in the Rebel service and that, although she had received letters from them, she had never written to either of them.[109]

Left: An 1854 daguerreotype of Marion Vail. *Missouri Historical Society, St. Louis.*

Right: Confederate mail runner Absalom Grimes, whose principal assistants included Marion Vail. *Missouri Historical Society, St. Louis.*

Continuing her statement, Mrs. Vail admitted,

> *Letters have been sent south through my instrumentality. From whom and to whom, and by what means they came to me and were sent by me, I do not wish to tell—but the means I will tell. They came to me with letters and numbers to which I had a key. Without the key, you could not tell who they were for. They came in two envelopes, the outside one being addressed to me by this key, the inside one having the name of the person for whom intended.*

Marion said, as far as she knew, no Confederate letters had been sent in or out of St. Louis during the previous two months. Then she resumed her description of how the mail-running scheme worked. "Grimes made this key," she explained, "and it was left at my house, and I have sent many letters through its devices and received them and distributed them by mail and otherwise. I did not harbor Grimes but would have done so if my husband had not forbidden me to do so. I fear him more than the authorities."[110]

After her interrogation, Marion was ordered to be banished to the South and to be committed to the McLure Female Prison on Chestnut Street pending execution of the sentence. However, the next day, May 19, 1863, she was paroled to her home on Morgan Street, between Fourteenth and Fifteenth Streets, under the condition that she would not leave the house until further orders from the provost marshal general's office.[111]

The arrest of Mrs. Vail caused Union authorities to question her husband's loyalty as well. However, the investigation of Corra Vail was quickly dropped after four reliable citizens gave separate statements on May 19 affirming that he was an upholder of the Union.[112]

On the morning of May 20, Marion, in an effort to have her parole extended, sent a Union man to the office of the judge advocate, Major Lucien Eaton, asking him to vouch for her, and later that day, Eaton wrote to Colonel Dick on Mrs. Vail's behalf. Eaton said he had visited with Mrs. Vail about six weeks earlier, when she had called at his office on behalf of an acquaintance seeking return of a slave who had been emancipated because of her acquaintance's alleged disloyalty. Marion freely admitted at the time that she was "an awful rebel," but after a lengthy conversation with her, Eaton became impressed by her honor and her candor, qualities he said he rarely saw in Rebels. Eaton thought Mrs. Vail would keep the terms of any parole that might be granted to her. He concluded by assuring Dick that he was not trying to interfere in the legal proceedings against Marion and was not asking a favor but simply stating a fact.[113]

The next day, May 21, Marion appealed to both Colonel Dick and department commander John M. Schofield, asking that her order of banishment be changed to the state of New Jersey instead of the South. After checking with the provost marshal's office to make sure there was no reason that the request could not be granted, General Schofield ruled that she should be permitted to go to New Jersey with the stipulation that she not return during the rebellion.[114]

On May 25, Mary Byrnes, a citizen of St. Louis, gave a statement to Lieutenant Patrick of the provost marshal's office, the same officer whom Hattie Snodgrass had allegedly called "a Lincoln hireling." Mrs. Byrnes said she knew of a Rebel spy in the city and also a Rebel mail carrier. Although Byrnes did not directly accuse Marion Vail, she did mention her name. Apparently that was enough to raise suspicion in Schofield's mind, because, on May 27, he revoked his previous order allowing Marion to go to New Jersey and ordered that she be sent south at first opportunity.[115]

While Marion waited to be sent south, the provost marshal's office continued collecting evidence against her. Elmisa Parker, an old schoolmate of Absalom Grimes, said she had no knowledge of Mrs. Vail or anybody else helping Grimes escape from Gratiot Street Prison, but she had heard Mrs. Vail admit to harboring him after his escape. She knew that Mrs. Vail generally spoke in favor of the South, but she could not recall the specific language she used.[116]

Mary E. Hicks, matron of the McLure Female Prison, was interviewed on May 29, the same day as Ms. Parker. Hicks said that Marion Vail, while under her supervision, was "one of the most rebellious and insulting prisoners" in her charge. In fact, she thought Mrs. Vail was "the worst—save Mrs. Sappington." (St. Louis County resident Drusella Sappington was ordered banished in the fall of 1862 and had finally been shipped south with Hattie Snodgrass and others just two weeks before Mary Hicks gave her statement.) Mrs. Hicks felt Mrs. Vail's "whole conduct was very riotous and abusive to the Government." Marion "did not think it right for the darned abolition Government to put any 'Darned' old Union hags over decent people. I suppose, in fact I know, that she meant me when she said 'old Union hags.'"[117]

Speaking of Marion Vail, Mrs. Hicks continued,

> *I have heard her say, while in prison, that she rode, disguised, 4 days and nights, to assist Ab Grimes, the Rebel mail carrier, to get outside the Union lines, that she concealed him here in the city after his escape, that he took dinner and supper with her, and that she would ride & disguise herself again to assist him or any other rebel to escape from the "darned" abolitionists. She said that she also assisted him in getting out of the prison and gloried in it and would do it again, said she knew that the Government knew it and that that was the reason she acknowledged it. That she and her husband differed on politics and consequently she desired to go south. Her whole conversations and actions were very unladylike, saying that few, if any, of the Union ladies were decent.*[118]

Absalom Grimes's memoirs tend to confirm Mrs. Hicks's accusations concerning Mrs. Vail's involvement in his escape from Gratiot. Certainly, Mrs. Hicks's charges appear closer to the truth than Mrs. Vail's denials nine days earlier. Grimes recollected that the day before his escape he sent word through Marion Vail to Lizzie Pickering that, if all went as planned, he would be at Mrs. Pickering's house late the following night. After his escape on October 2, 1862, he showed up at Lizzie's house about midnight, and he met Marion the next day. On the night of October 5, Marion and another woman escorted the escaped prisoner out of St. Louis to the home of a Southern sympathizer in the suburbs.[119]

Three days after Ms. Parker and Mrs. Hicks gave their statements, Marion Vail was banished to the South as an enemy of the U.S. government. Sixteen other prisoners and five family members who requested to go along with their banished loved ones were sent south at the same time. The exiles left St. Louis on June 1, 1863, headed down the Mississippi River aboard the *City of Alton* steamboat, accompanied by a Union escort commanded by Captain J.M. Adams of the First Missouri Cavalry. They were delivered into Confederate custody at Satartia, Mississippi, on June 13. A month or so later, Absalom Grimes met Mrs. Vail in Yazoo City, Mississippi, and escorted her and two or three other women to Georgia. During her sojourn in the South, according to Grimes, Mrs. Vail often socialized with Confederate officers and was a great hit among them.[120]

In the summer of 1863, Corra O. Vail applied to Union authorities to allow his wife to return to her family in Missouri. The secretary of war approved the request on September 12, and Marion started north shortly afterward. Years later, Grimes remembered escorting Mrs. Vail from Demopolis, Alabama, by way of Grenada, Mississippi, to Memphis on her return trip to Missouri.[121]

On reaching Missouri, Mrs. Vail was required to resume the conditions of her previous parole, remaining at her home in St. Louis. In March 1864, at Mr. Vail's request, the parole was amended to allow Marion and her children to live in Warren County with the stipulation that she report periodically by letter.[122]

In late March, Marion was summoned back to St. Louis to testify as a defense witness in the trial of Absalom Grimes, who had recently been recaptured. Grimes was convicted as a spy and sentenced to hang. He was later seriously wounded while attempting yet another escape, and still later he had his sentence commuted by President Lincoln.[123]

On May 27, 1864, Corra Vail again appealed to Union authorities on his wife's behalf, this time seeking to have her parole extended to include the entire state of Missouri. Provost Marshal General Sanderson asked Lieutenant Patrick, one of his assistants, to provide him a summary of Mrs. Vail's case so that he could make an informed decision on Corra Vail's latest request. In a letter accompanying the file on Marion that Patrick forwarded to Sanderson, the lieutenant explained that Mrs. Vail had been allowed to return to Missouri under the condition that she take an oath of allegiance to the United States but that, on reaching St. Louis, she had reported to the provost marshal's office that she had been accused as a Union spy while she was in the South and had been required to take an oath to the

Rebel government, thereby preventing her from now taking one to the U.S. government. Marion was, therefore, allowed to go to her home on parole without taking the oath. Patrick had since learned through Absalom Grimes, after his recapture, that, although Mrs. Vail was indeed arrested by Confederate authorities in Mississippi, she had been released without having to take an oath. Mrs. Vail was never in danger during her sojourn in the South, Patrick told Sanderson, and, in fact, "the officers were all in her power." Patrick considered her "the worst rebel in town."[124]

Based on the file in Mrs. Vail's case and Lieutenant Patrick's report, Sanderson recommended against granting Corra Vail's request, and General Rosecrans, therefore, denied it.[125]

In early August 1864, Mrs. Vail petitioned Union authorities to be allowed to come to St. Louis to visit her aged, ailing mother, who had recently become paralyzed and was not expected to live long. Although Sanderson observed at the time that Mrs. Vail's history was "a bad one for loyalty," permission was granted for her to come to St. Louis for three days, provided she report to provost marshal's office immediately on her arrival.[126]

On February 2, 1865, Corra Vail again applied to have the terms of his wife's parole amended. He asked that she be allowed to live in St. Louis because his business confined him to the city and he, therefore, rarely got to see his family. He also said that his children did not live close enough to a schoolhouse in Warren County to attend school and that they needed to be in St. Louis, where they would have better educational opportunities. Vail assured Colonel Baker, the new provost marshal general, that he was a loyal Union man who had served as an officer in the Enrolled Missouri Militia and that his wife had strictly complied with the terms of her parole.[127]

Baker immediately launched an investigation to determine whether the charges against Mrs. Vail were of such a character as to allow the parole to be granted. William B. Brooke, who lived near Marion Vail in Warren County, testified that he had heard her speak in favor of the South. The previous October, a band of bushwhackers had visited his neighborhood, stealing from Union citizens, and they had come and gone by way of Mrs. Vail's house, even though it was a quarter of a mile out of the way. When asked about the incident, Mrs. Vail had claimed that the guerrillas stole some blankets from her as well, but Brooke and other Union citizens suspected Mrs. Vail had brought the blankets from St. Louis and given them to the bushwhackers. A week later, another party of Rebels under Colonel Caleb Dorsey had come through the neighborhood and stopped at Mrs. Vail's house. Marion claimed the Confederates only stopped to examine

Among Marion Vail's Confederate friends was Colonel Caleb Dorsey. *Missouri Historical Society, St. Louis.*

her parole papers, but Brooke accused her of mounting a horse after they left and riding to a railroad where Dorsey and his men were tearing up the tracks. Marion supposedly greeted Dorsey with a warm handshake and persuaded him to return two horses that his men had taken from a friend of hers. On three separate occasions, Brooke added, Mrs. Vail had hosted a sewing bee, but each time only the same four women attended. Since all four were considered Southern sympathizers, it was assumed they were making clothes for Rebel soldiers. In addition, during the winter, Mrs. Vail had been visited three times "in the absence of her husband" by "strange men." When asked their identity, Mrs. Vail had said the men were friends of hers from St. Louis. No doubt one of them was Absalom Grimes, who later recalled visiting Marion Vail in Warren County at Christmastime of 1864.[128]

Brooke's wife, Eliza, testified that Marion Vail had come to her house during General Sterling Price's invasion of Missouri in the fall of 1864 and that Mrs. Vail was "delighted about Price being in Missouri." Marion allegedly said that she considered the men of Price's army her "warmest friends" and she only hoped she lived long enough to see her son join Price. In addition, Eliza stated that a "mulatto" woman who lived near Mrs. Vail had reported that Marion blamed William Brooke for Federal soldiers having come to her house during the winter and that she'd said that if bushwhackers ever came into the neighborhood again, she would have Brooke paid back.[129]

Corra Vail's latest request to have the conditions of his wife's parole amended, like his previous one, was not approved, and she remained in Warren County. She returned to St. Louis at the end of the war and was living there in 1870. She and Corra were still living in St. Louis, in the Sixth Ward, ten years later. Their son and daughter were both married, and their families were living in the same household with Corra and Marion. By 1900, Corra had died, and Marion was living in the Twenty-First Ward with her daughter, Cora Albright, and Cora's family.[130]

Even after the Civil War had long ended, Marion Vail remained an ardent supporter of the South. According to Grimes:

> *Until the day of her death at the age of eighty-two years she never realized that the war was over, as her spirit of patriotism and warm love for the South never waned and she was fond of relating war stories in her interesting way to her many friends of all ages. She was popular with young people as well as with older ones, and was a welcome guest in a large number of homes. She never grew feeble, but continued active until within a few weeks of her death in 1907. She was an ardent member of the Third Baptist Church of St. Louis and was a helpful, idolized teacher of a large class of young men. She was also a loved and valued member of the M.A.E. McLure Chapter of the United Daughters of the Confederacy.*[131]

8

Mary Susan F. Cleveland

A Veritable "She Adder"

What was it with the lady schoolteachers of Missouri and their Southern sympathies? No fewer than three of the women whose stories are chronicled in previous chapters were schoolteachers, and Mary S.F. Cleveland was yet another young teacher banished from the state because of her disloyalty. Like the other three, Mary was more stubborn in her opposition to the Union than the simple country girls of rural Missouri who were arrested primarily for feeding and harboring guerrillas.

Born in November 1832 in Virginia, Mary came to Missouri with her parents and siblings about 1840 and settled in the Huntsville area of Randolph County. When the war broke out, two of her younger brothers, Charles and Benjamin, joined the Southern forces. Older brother John stayed in Randolph County but was required to take an oath of allegiance in March 1862. Later the same year, Ben died of disease in Mississippi while serving in the Confederate army.[132]

In early January 1863, Mary moved to Auburn in Lincoln County to teach school. Alone and away from family, she soon started exchanging letters with loved ones and friends. Unfortunately for her, she wasn't always discreet in what she said or with whom she corresponded.[133]

About the same time as Mary's move to Auburn, her brother John was arrested, apparently for refusing to enlist in the Enrolled Missouri Militia, and he was imprisoned in St. Louis. In February 1863, his mother, Jane Cleveland, wrote to Brigadier General Thomas Bartholow, district commander of the militia, pleading that, if John were released, he would take the oath and leave Missouri for another Union state but that he would not join the Union army and fight against his brother. Whether Jane's request was granted is not clear.[134]

Sometime about the middle of May 1863, one of Mary's letters was confiscated by Union soldiers at her mother's home in Randolph County, and it sparked an investigation that turned up several more questionable letters in Mary's and Jane's possession. Mary, still living in Lincoln County, was promptly arrested and taken to Troy. On May 19, General Bartholow had her and at least two of the suspicious letters transported to the provost marshal general's office in St. Louis. Over the next couple of days, additional evidence against Mary was forwarded from north Missouri, and she was interrogated on May 22.[135]

During the interview, Mary's examiner presented, one by one, the letters that had been confiscated as evidence against her and asked her to state whether she had written them or to otherwise identify them. Exhibit "A" was a letter to Sally (probably Mary's sister Sarah) with a dateline of March 30, 1863, Auburn, Missouri. The letter said two area young women, Misses Merriweather and Knight, had recently taken a bundle of letters to St. Louis for mailing south but were arrested before they could complete their errand. The letter writer feared she might soon be arrested, too, since she had helped gather the letters and had written a few of them. The writer also disparaged some Union men, declaring that the "N.S." in one of their names stood for "nasty" and "stinking." Although the letter was unsigned, it had been confiscated at Mary's mother's home at the same time as another letter that Mary had signed, and the handwriting in the two letters matched perfectly. Despite the evidence against her, Mary denied writing the letter or even knowing any young women named Knight or Merriweather.[136]

The letter marked Exhibit "B" was included as evidence primarily for the purposes of a handwriting comparison, because it was the letter that Mary had signed and that was found at the same time as Exhibit "A." Mary had written the Exhibit "B" letter to her mother on March 16 from Auburn. Except for a comment that the rector of the church she attended did "not pray for the president of the United States," the letter concerned commonplace news and inquiries about family and friends. Still, Mary declined to answer questions about it or to say who its recipient might have been, probably in an effort to shield her mother. She admitted, however, that she might eventually have to say who she thought wrote it.[137]

Exhibit "C" was a letter Mary had written to her mother from Auburn on January 31, 1863, not long after moving there from home. She told Jane she didn't know how long she would stay, because she'd already helped Isaac, a fugitive from Union justice, get out of Missouri, which was the main reason she'd gone to Auburn instead of Waverly to teach school. She dreaded facing her students, she said, because she thought they were too advanced for her limited education, and she expressed a desire to go back to school for more learning, because she supposed she would "teach the remnant of [her] days." Although the letter was signed "Mary," Mary Cleveland denied that she had written it.[138]

Exhibit "D" was an undated, unsigned letter that Mary had written to her mother in which she referred to young women who delivered letters to Southern soldiers and prisoners as "Sisters of Charity." Predictably, Mary declined to answer any questions about the letter.[139]

Exhibit "E" was the only letter presented to Mary that she was willing to talk about. She readily admitted it was a letter she had received from her brother Charles, who was then in Confederate service in Mississippi. It contained no particularly damning evidence against Mary, except that it suggested she was guilty of corresponding with the enemy. However, she

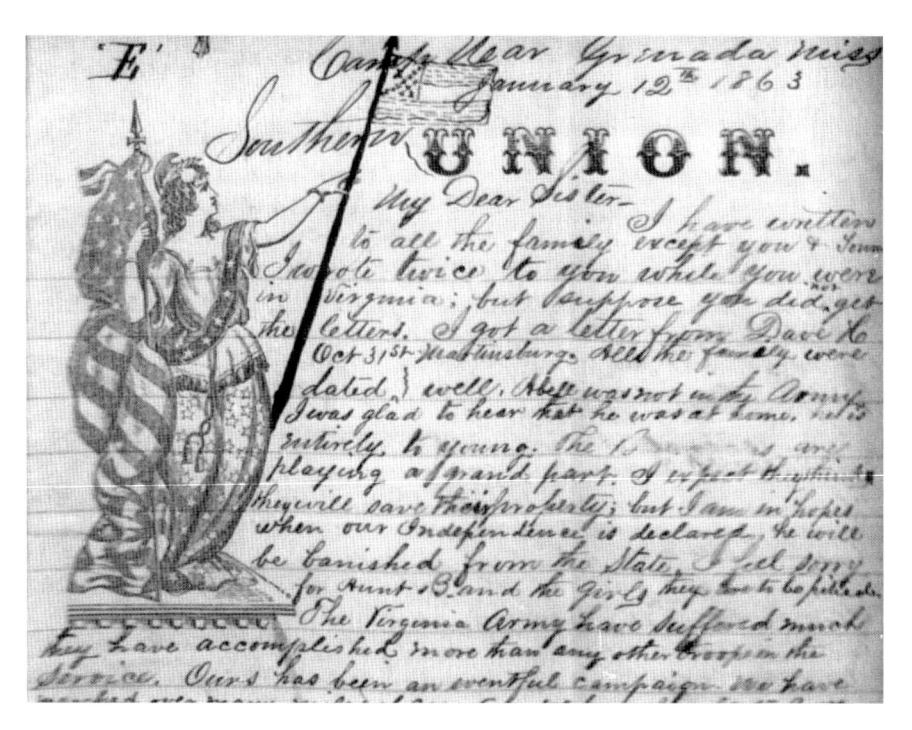

This letter from Charles Cleveland, dated January 12, 1863, was part of the evidence in the case against his sister Mary Cleveland. *Fold3.com*.

claimed the only letters she'd ever written to Rebel soldiers were not sent secretly but were sent under a flag of truce.[140]

Mary refused to swear an oath, but near the end of her examination, she reaffirmed that she knew nothing about Jennie Knight or Miss Merriweather taking Rebel mail to St. Louis and that she had not written any of the letters that had been shown to her during the interview. Of course, her examiner, Captain R.M. Swander, didn't believe her. He watched her sign the statement solemnly affirming that her answers were true, and he thought that "a more willful and malicious deception of her handwriting could not be had." Her refusal to answer questions was also very incriminating, and he ventured that she was "without a doubt guilty of all acts charged against her." Swander recommended her banishment "to the place where her affections yearn for.…Taking General Blunt as my authority," he concluded, "she is a veritable 'she adder.'" (This was a reference to a statement General James G. Blunt, stationed at Leavenworth, Kansas, had made a few days earlier. Recognizing the central role that women played in the Rebel uprising in Missouri, Blunt declared that "the bite of the she adder is as poisonous and productive of mischief as the bite of any other venomous reptile."[141])

Suspicion also fell on Mary's mother because of letters she had written to Charles, but two Union soldiers, who were well acquainted with Jane, told General Bartholow that she was sometimes subject to "derangement of the mind." He therefore did not press the matter, and no charges were filed against her.[142]

Mary, however, was banished to the South, despite pleas on her behalf from Randolph County citizens and from her sister Sarah, a St. Louis resident. On May 27, Mary was paroled to go back to Randolph and Lincoln Counties to make preparations for the journey south. In accordance with the terms of the parole, she promptly returned to St. Louis, and on June 1, she left for Dixie aboard the *City of Alton* steamer along with Marion Vail.[143]

Sometime in the early fall of 1863, Mary accompanied Mrs. Vail from Mississippi back to Tennessee, thinking her banishment order had been lifted, only to learn on reaching Memphis that the release from exile applied only to Mrs. Vail. Back in the Deep South in mid-December, Mary wrote to Willis M. Reynolds, a prominent citizen of Lincoln County who had taken an interest in her case at the time of her banishment. Mary thanked him for that kindness and asked whether he might intercede on her behalf once again. Even though she was among friends and had plenty to eat, she was anxious to see her widowed mother, who was melancholy and deranged by the events that had befallen her family. Mary said she would not swear an

General James G. Blunt considered the bite of "she adders" like Mary Cleveland just as poisonous as that of any other "venomous reptile." *Library of Congress.*

oath of allegiance to the Union or any other government, including the Confederacy, but that she would pledge not to do anything to harm the Federal cause if she were allowed to return.[144]

Reynolds, in turn, wrote to Provost Marshal General James Broadhead in late December pleading at length for Mary to be allowed to return to Missouri. Although she could not, as a matter of religious principle, swear an oath to a government, Reynolds knew her to be an honest and upstanding young woman who was not outspoken in political matters and who, he was sure, would honor her pledge not to do anything against the Federal cause.

The main reason she had been banished in the first place rather than given a lesser punishment, Reynolds felt, stemmed from an argument she had gotten into with Captain James Dwight, acting provost marshal general at the time of her arrest. Reynolds was there when the heated exchange took place, and he thought Dwight was as much to blame as Miss Cleveland. Reynolds's letter was endorsed by three other Lincoln County citizens, who expressed their strong agreement with it.[145]

Whether Reynolds's letter had any effect in getting Mary's banishment order revoked is not certain, but a notation added by an unnamed Union officer to the letter's cover sheet suggests not. The unknown officer's assessment of Mary's appeal was that she considered herself "to [sic] good a Rebel" to take the oath.[146]

At some point, Mary did come back to Missouri, and she lived there the rest of her life. She moved to St. Louis and, in keeping with the prediction expressed in her January 1863 letter to her mother, spent the rest of her days teaching school and serving as an assistant principal. She died of cancer on July 15, 1898, and was buried in St. Louis's Bellefontaine Cemetery.[147]

9

The Blennerhassett Sisters

Uncompromising Rebel Sympathizers

When Therese Blennerhassett was banished to the South in the fall of 1863, her sister Annie B. Martin was granted permission to accompany her under the same terms that governed Therese's banishment order. In reporting the banishments, the *St. Louis Daily Missouri Republican* called Blennerhassett "an inveterate and uncompromising rebel sympathizer," but before the Civil War was over, Mrs. Martin would eventually end up in more serious trouble.[148]

Born in New York, Annie and Therese were collateral descendants of Harman Blennerhassett, implicated in Aaron Burr's treasonous scheme against the United States in the early 1800s. Cousins of Addie Haynes (see chapter 4), the sisters came to St. Louis in 1842 with their parents, Richard and Therese Blennerhassett. Annie, the oldest daughter, married George F. Martin at St. Louis in 1853. Annie's father, who was a noted criminal lawyer, died in 1857, and her husband died about the same time. Widowed and twenty-four years old, Annie was living back home in 1860; nineteen-year-old Therese was single and also living with her mother.[149]

At the very beginning of the war, Annie and Therese's brother Edward was one of the state militiamen captured by U.S. forces at Camp Jackson, and he later joined the Confederate army. His sisters exchanged letters with him and other Rebel soldiers even after such correspondence was banned early in the war. The sisters supported the Southern war effort in other ways, too, or at least tried to. Sometime in 1862 or very early in 1863, Therese requested that she and Annie be allowed to visit their Southern friends in the Myrtle Street Military Prison. Therese assured the provost marshal general that their motives were honorable and purely benevolent, but whether the request was granted is unknown.[150]

In late March 1863, Therese went south at her own request, and very shortly afterward, at least three of her and Annie's letters fell into the hands of Union authorities. Annie was questioned about them at the provost marshal general's office on April 1. She said she had one brother in the Confederate army. She was delighted to add that she would "rather have him a teamster in the Rebel army than a major general in the Union Army." He was not in Tennessee but was "coming back with Old Price." Asked when General Price was coming back, she said probably this coming summer, but she was "not at liberty to tell the *exact date*." Annie admitted writing to her brother many times but declined to answer questions about how the letters were mailed or received. Shown three letters, she declined to identify them, despite the fact that Therese's signature was on two of them and she herself had likely written the other one.[151]

There's no evidence that any action was taken against Annie at the time of her examination in April 1863. In September of that year, however, her sister Therese was arrested when she returned to St. Louis without a pass.[152]

Therese refused to take an oath but was released on parole to St. Louis with orders to report by letter to Provost Marshal General James O. Broadhead every week. In October, the limits of her parole were changed to Alton, Illinois, and after she'd been in Alton a few weeks, she requested that she be allowed to visit St. Louis for a day or two to purchase clothing and other needed items. The request was granted, but it wasn't long before Therese was headed south again, and this time not by choice.[153]

Therese's stubborn refusal to take the oath of allegiance was seemingly the lone cause of her banishment. According to one report, her friends had made every effort to get her to swear allegiance, but in vain. Annie requested to accompany her sister, and they left aboard the *Luminary* on November 22 with a number of other exiles. Those accompanying the exiles by request were under the same obligations that governed the persons banished, meaning they could not return during the war.[154]

But that didn't stop Annie from coming back to St. Louis less than a year later. On September 18, 1864, she started from Mississippi, where she and Therese had been staying, and she arrived in St. Louis on September 27. She stopped at a friend's house on South Thirteenth Street and sent word to her mother, who was staying in Alton, Illinois, that she was back home.[155]

Lieutenant Ed Blennerhassett, Annie and Therese's brother, pictured here with fellow Confederate officer Overton Barrett. It is not known which man is which. *Missouri Historical Society, St. Louis.*

Union provost marshal general James O. Broadhead released Therese Blennerhassett on parole in the fall of 1863. *Missouri Historical Society, St. Louis.*

She might have gone unnoticed if she'd come back only to see her mother, as she claimed, but that wasn't the case. While Annie was still in the South, Confederate captain W.H. Murrell, who knew Annie was preparing to leave for Missouri, had sent her a letter with news about himself and his brother, also a Southern soldier, with a request that she share the news with his wife and other family members when she got to Missouri. Annie planned to do just that, and she'd even brought Murrell's letter along with her.

On September 23, she wrote from St. Louis to Murrell's wife, enclosing the captain's letter. The next day, she wrote a letter to "My dear friends," passing along news from Mississippi and inviting them, if they wanted her to carry any news back there with her, to please write her in St. Louis in care of Miss Julia Butler as soon as possible, as she did not plan to stay long. She wanted to get back to Therese in Mississippi, and she also knew that, if she stayed in St. Louis long, she would be arrested because, as she told her friends, she was "here secretly."[156]

Unfortunately for Annie, her arrest came quicker than she probably anticipated. Her letters were intercepted by Union authorities in late September, and she was lodged in the St. Charles Street Female Prison on October 3, charged with violating her order of banishment. After examining the circumstances of her case, Judge Advocate Lucien Eaton recommended that she be tried by military commission.[157]

Annie gave a statement at or near the time of her arrest. She declared that she was a Southern woman and wished to see the Confederacy succeed but that she would not do anything to help the Rebel cause while she was within Federal lines. When in the South, though, she would do all she could to help the Confederacy, because she believed it was in the right. She said that, if she were released, she would return to the South. When she came to St. Louis, the only letters she brought were unsealed, because she knew she might get in trouble for bringing sealed letters.[158]

On October 18, acting provost marshal general Joseph Darr Jr., in forwarding Annie's file to General Rosecrans's headquarters, suggested that

Annie should be made an example of. Three days later, Annie was moved to the Gratiot Street Female Prison after the St. Charles Street Prison was closed.[159]

At her trial on October 26, Annie was convicted on the single charge of violating her order of banishment, and she was sentenced to imprisonment for the duration of the war. About three weeks later, she was transferred from Gratiot Street Female Prison to the Alton (Illinois) Military Prison across the Mississippi River.[160]

On November 26, President Lincoln took an interest in Annie's case, presumably at the urging of her St. Louis friends. He wired General Rosecrans asking what the charges and evidence against Annie were, and Rosecrans replied, explaining that she had returned from banishment without permission, was a Rebel sympathizer, and had vowed to return to the South if released.[161]

Judge Advocate Lucien Eaton recommended that Annie B. Martin be tried by military commission. *Missouri Historical Society, St. Louis.*

Two or three weeks after Annie arrived at the Alton prison, fellow prisoner Griffin Frost, a Confederate captain, had what he called "a pleasant conversation" with her. She told him that she'd had "a hard time during her imprisonment" and had occasionally been "treated very badly." Later, Frost got to know Annie better and met her mother and her sister Alice when they came to visit.[162]

Occasionally, Annie was allowed to visit her mother outside the prison, and her mother, who came often, was always allowed to bring medicine and other "little favors" that the prisoners would not otherwise have had access to. Frost thought Annie was "a very kind and amiable lady."[163]

On February 24, 1865, General Grenville M. Dodge, who'd replaced Rosecrans as commanding general of the department, remitted Annie's prison sentence and banished her to the South. Preparatory to her leaving, she was transferred to the Gratiot Street Prison, from where, on the twenty-eighth, she wrote to Nannie Douthitt, a fellow inmate back at Alton, detailing her arrival the night before and her ordeal at having to sleep in a room without heat.[164]

Annie left St. Louis on March 3, and on March 9, she wrote to Captain Frost from Pine Bluff, Arkansas. Already a "travelled rebel," she was waiting to "go out under a flag of truce," and she planned to accompany two families

Map of St. Louis showing location of Civil War military prisons. The Alton Military Prison was north of St. Louis across the Mississippi River. *Author's collection.*

who were going to Texas. But she meant to reunite with Therese as soon as she could after that, and she also wanted to see General Price. So, as she told Frost, "My journey is only just commencing."[165]

After the war, both Annie and Therese returned to St. Louis and moved back in with their mother. Therese became a schoolteacher, and both she and Annie were active in St. Louis social circles. Annie died in 1887 and was buried at Bellefontaine Cemetery. In 1890, Therese was granted a court order changing her name to Therese Blennerhassett-Adams. She explained that she had married a man named Adams twenty years earlier but that the marriage was kept secret because of her family's strong opposition to it.

Annie Martin was imprisoned at the Alton (Illinois) Military Prison in the fall of 1864. *Missouri Historical Society, St. Louis.*

Adams died shortly after the marriage, and even after their daughter was born some months later, the marriage was kept secret from those outside the family, who were told the daughter was adopted. In the early 1890s, Therese was active in organizing and promoting the St. Louis Exposition. She died in 1913 and, like Annie, was buried at Bellefontaine Cemetery.[166]

10

Pauline White

Sentenced to Hard Labor

Nineteen-year-old Pauline White's first brush with Union authority came in 1863, when she was charged with hurrahing for the Confederacy and was compelled to take an oath of allegiance. It wasn't until the next year, though, when she broke her oath, that she got into real trouble. She claimed she'd been misled by the "treasonable advice of friends," but that wasn't enough to keep Pauline from being one of only a handful of women sent to the Missouri State Penitentiary during the Civil War for their disloyal activities.[167]

Sarah Pauline White was born in Tennessee in July 1844, the third of nine children of Dr. Terrell C. and Sarah Elizabeth White. The family moved to southeast Missouri in the mid-1850s and settled in rural Greenville, the Wayne County seat, where Dr. White set up his medical practice.[168]

By the fall of 1863, the Union had solid control of Missouri, but Greenville, like most of the rural areas of the state, still had more than its share of Southern sympathizers. Among them were the White sisters, whose older brother had joined the Confederate army the previous year. One day in early October 1863, a detail of Union soldiers was marching through Greenville, and a number of onlookers, including Pauline and two of her sisters, had gathered to watch the procession. As the Federal soldiers paraded through the town, Pauline, older sister Eveline, and younger sister Arabella began taunting them and hurrahing for the Confederacy. Family tradition holds that Eveline instigated the scene and that she and her sisters considered it little more than a lark, but Federal authorities failed to see the humor in their behavior.[169]

On October 15, Clinton Fisk, commanding general in Southeast Missouri, ordered that the daughters of Dr. White be arrested and sent to Fisk's headquarters at Pilot Knob. "Their names are Evaline, Paulina, and Arabella," the general said. "Tell them to prepare their clothing for a journey southward by way of the Mississippi River. They shall be sent to the people and region they hurrah for. Let there be no delay. Let them be well treated."[170]

Dr. White made the trip to Pilot Knob with his daughters, and all four were charged there on October 19 with disloyalty. The threat to send the White sisters south, however, was apparently a bluff meant to scare them, because they were simply required to sign oaths of allegiance and then released. Pauline was described in Union records at the time as standing five feet tall, with dark hair and dark eyes. Dr. White was required to sign an oath of allegiance, pledge to abstain from alcohol during the rebellion, and give bond. He was then paroled to the limits of Wayne County with instructions to split up his daughters. Evaline was sent to stay with relatives in Arkansas, Arabella went to live with relatives in Illinois, and Pauline stayed home to help her father as a clerk in his medical practice.[171]

Charles Dekalb White, Pauline's older brother and a sergeant in Confederate colonel Timothy Reeves's Fifteenth Cavalry, was captured in Ripley County during the so-called Christmas Day Massacre of December 25, 1863, when Reeves's camp was overrun by Federal soldiers. White was taken to St. Louis, and he died there in the Gratiot Street Prison hospital of a lung ailment on January 16, 1864. After word of his death reached the White family in February, Pauline wrote a letter to Drury Poston, a soldier in Reeves's command, informing Dekalb's comrades of his death. She sent it by a Greenville teacher named Reeves (no relation to Timothy Reeves) for delivery to Poston, who was in Arkansas with Tim Reeves's regiment.[172]

Pauline White is shown a few years after the Civil War. *Courtesy of David Bollinger, president of the Wayne County Historical Society.*

The letter made it as far as Cherokee Bay, Arkansas, before it was discovered at a house there and confiscated by a Federal scouting party sent out from Patterson, Missouri. Had Pauline quit writing after informing Poston of her brother's death, the letter might have been left undisturbed, but she had expressed some disloyal sentiments

> **OATH OF ALLEGIANCE.**
>
> I, Malina White, of Wayne County, State of Missouri do hereby solemnly swear that I will bear true allegiance to the United States, and support and sustain the Constitution and laws thereof; that I will maintain the National Sovereignty paramount to that of all State, County or Confederate powers; that I will discourage, discountenance, and forever oppose secession, rebellion and the disintegration of the Federal Union; that I disclaim and denounce all faith and fellowship with the so-called Confederate Armies, and pledge my honor, my property, and my life, to the sacred performance of this my solemn Oath of Allegiance to the Government of the United States of America.
>
> Pauline White
>
> Subscribed and sworn to before me this 19th day of October 1863, at Pilot Knob Mo

Pauline White's oath, taken in the fall of 1863. *Fold3.com.*

near the end of the missive. She asked God to bless Poston and "all the rest of the boys" and then concluded, "Long live the Rebels, peace and comfort rest upon their heads."[173]

Pauline was arrested at her home on May 28, 1864, and taken to Patterson, ten miles from Greenville. She was paroled and sent back home while the assistant provost marshal at Patterson sought clarification on whether corresponding with the enemy after having taken an oath of allegiance was sufficient grounds to send the prisoner to St. Louis. After receiving assurance that sending a letter to a Southern soldier clandestinely was, indeed, sufficient grounds, the assistant provost marshal had Pauline brought back to Greenville on June 12 and forwarded to St. Louis the next day by way of Pilot Knob. She arrived in St. Louis on the fifteenth and was interrogated the same day.[174]

Pauline admitted during questioning that she had previously taken an oath of allegiance but claimed not to know it was binding. She also admitted writing and sending the letter to Drury Poston. In addition to the letter informing Pauline and her family of Dekalb White's death, the family had received two other letters, addressed to men in Reeves's command, from a Confederate prisoner captured at the same time as Dekalb, and Pauline said she had forwarded those at the same time she sent her letter to Poston. She had met Reeves, the Greenville teacher, on a road just outside town on March 19 and given him the letters for delivery, since she understood that he was preparing to go south. She said she had never sent any other letters to Southern soldiers and didn't know of anyone who had. She'd had no other dealings with Reeves, the carrier, before or since March 19. She admitted some of Tim Reeves's men had visited her home before she took the oath but not since.[175]

Charged with violating her oath of allegiance and corresponding with the enemy, Pauline was lodged in the St. Charles Street Prison, which had a reputation for unsanitary conditions and mistreatment of prisoners. Sometime not long after her arrival, Pauline clashed with Margaret Dickson, the prison keeper's wife, when Mrs. Dickson tried to make Pauline give up her clean, new comforter for an old one. Pauline refused, saying the old blanket was "too dirty for a white person or a negro to sleep under." Mrs. Dickson threw the old blanket in Pauline's face, and Pauline promptly told her that if she did it again, Pauline would knock her down. Mrs. Dickson jerked the new blanket out of Pauline's hands and dared her to try, calling Pauline a "lousy, dirty hussy who shouldn't have anything to sleep on." Mrs. Dickson then locked Pauline in her room on half rations without toilet facilities and allowed her to clean herself and her room only when a Union inspector was scheduled to visit.[176]

At her trial by military commission on June 28, 1864, Pauline pleaded guilty to both charges against her but maintained that she had not intended for her letter to Poston "to give aid and comfort to the rebel enemies of the United States by furnishing them with intelligence," as specified in the second charge. She was sentenced "to be confined at hard labor during the war in the Missouri State Penitentiary." Exactly what constituted hard labor for a female prisoner and why Pauline's sentence was seemingly harsher than those of other women convicted of similar offenses are unanswered questions.[177]

The sentence was promulgated on August 17, and Pauline was transferred to the state prison in Jefferson City on August 24. Six months later, on February 19, 1865, she wrote to General John Pope, commanding the Military Division of Missouri, requesting a remission of her sentence. She said she was "earnestly sorry" for her past disloyalty and asked that she be allowed to take an oath of allegiance and be banished to the state of Indiana. She hoped Pope would "pardon the error of an unfortunate girl in yielding to the treasonable advice of friends." She promised to pray for Pope's welfare and the success of his cause.[178]

Missouri legislator and Union officer James McMurtry added his endorsement to Pauline's letter. A resident of Wayne County, McMurtry said he had known Pauline for a long time and thought she was a young lady of "estimable character" in every respect except for her disloyal sentiments. McMurtry thought Pauline was now truly repentant for her past deeds and would conduct herself in the future in a respectable and loyal manner. He asked that her request be granted.[179]

General John Pope, to whom Pauline White appealed for clemency. *Missouri Historical Society, St. Louis.*

Pope was apparently unmoved by both Pauline's letter and the lawmaker's intervention, because she remained in prison another four months. No action was taken in Pauline's case until Missouri governor Thomas Fletcher also got involved. In early June, he wrote to Pope vouching for McMurtry, who had renewed his petition on Pauline's behalf. Fletcher said that he, too, personally knew Pauline White and knew she was from a good family and had "an unsullied reputation" except in this one matter. Pope apparently forwarded Fletcher's appeal to Washington, D.C., because on June 10, General Ulysses S Grant, commanding the U.S. Army, directed Pope to release Pauline White in accordance with President Andrew Johnson's order, dated May 27, 1865, discharging all persons sentenced to prison by military tribunals during the war. Pauline finally walked out of the Missouri State Penitentiary a free woman on June 23, more than two months after the Civil War had officially ended.[180]

Pauline reunited with her mother and sisters in Illinois and then returned home to Greenville. Later, she lived in Randolph County, Arkansas, where, in 1873, she married Oliver Dalton, widower of her sister Evaline. The couple came back to Greenville and took up residence on the old White farm. Pauline raised Evaline's daughter as her own and gave birth to at least two more children. Throughout the late 1800s and into the early 1900s, Pauline was active in the social and church life of Greenville and was one of the most prominent women in the community. The 1888 *History of Southeast Missouri* briefly profiled Pauline, recalling that she was "subjected to unusual indignities" during the Civil War, including a sentence of hard labor in the state prison after a "mock trial" at St. Louis. Pauline died in 1936 at the age of ninety-two.[181]

11

Martha Cassell

A Very Rank Rebel

On the morning of February 6, 1864, a long list of names to whom unclaimed letters at the St. Louis Post Office were addressed was published in the *Daily Missouri Democrat*. One of the names was Martha Washington, an alias that twenty-three-year old Martha Cassell had adopted to communicate with Confederate prisoners and soldiers. After reading the notice in the newspaper, the black-eyed, black-haired Cassell headed for the post office later that morning. Unbeknownst to her, she was walking into a trap.[182]

Martha was born in Marion County, Missouri, about 1840 to dentist John F. Cassell and his wife, Ann. Shortly after Martha's birth, the family returned to Maryland, where Martha's older siblings had been born. The Cassells remained long enough for two younger children to be born before coming back to Marion County in the late 1840s and taking up residence outside Palmyra, where Dr. Cassell had his dental practice.[183]

Martha, or Mattie, as she was often called, went to St. Louis in October 1863 to live with an older sister, Mary Squire. It was during her stay in St. Louis that Martha began sending and receiving letters to and from Confederate prisoners and soldiers. One of the men with whom she regularly communicated was John W. Priest, a Confederate lieutenant colonel who had recently been captured and lodged in the Gratiot Street Prison in St. Louis. Prior to the war, Priest lived in Marion County close to Martha's old neighborhood, and much of their correspondence concerned mutual acquaintances. Priest was not married, but there is no suggestion of romance between him and Martha. In fact, in one letter he referred to her as his niece, although that might have been a pretense to misdirect snooping eyes, because there seems to be no evidence that the two were, in fact, related by blood. Mostly, Priest addressed Martha as a friend, and he often thanked her for her kind concern for him during his ordeal. The overall content of Priest's letters to Martha was innocuous. In one letter, he even warned her against sending forbidden items to him. Martha's letters to Priest do not survive, but it wasn't her correspondence with him that got her into serious trouble anyway.[184]

It was her letters to and from a young man named Lewis Rogers, alias F.M. Kaylor, that caused Martha trouble. A native of Boone County, Rogers had served in the Missouri State Guard early in the war. In March 1862, he'd taken an oath of allegiance at Columbia, but that didn't stop him from taking to the bush on behalf of the Confederate cause. He stayed with his uncle in Marion County in 1863, at which time he likely became acquainted with Martha Cassell. He was captured in St. Louis in mid-September 1863, accused of being a notorious guerrilla and a "hard case," and lodged in the Myrtle Street Prison. When Martha reached St. Louis the next month, she began a correspondence with Rogers at the request of his uncle, who'd asked her before she left Marion County to check on the young man once she got to the city. Rogers escaped sometime in November. After his escape, he roamed into northern Missouri and then ventured into Clark County, Illinois, where he tried to incite "an insurrection among Copperheads." (*Copperhead* was a pejorative term for a Northern citizen who nominally favored the Union but who opposed the war.) While Rogers was on the lam, he resumed writing to Martha Cassell. Their exchange of letters while he was in prison was through legal, military channels, but by corresponding with a Rebel fugitive, Martha was now breaking the law.[185]

Rogers's latest letter to Martha, dated January 27, 1864, in Paris, Illinois, but postmarked Tuscumbia, Missouri, awaited Martha at the St. Louis Post Office on the morning of February 6. She had to pay a penny to pick it up. Although Rogers addressed Martha as "Dear Sister" in the salutation of the letter, she was not his sister. However, he did adopt almost a brotherly tone with little hint of romance. Like Priest, Rogers thanked Martha for the kindness and friendship she had shown him, especially when "disaster strickened around [him]." This was a reference to his imprisonment in St. Louis. He signed the letter "F.M. Kaylor."[186]

What Martha didn't know was that Union authorities had already been alerted that in early January a person living near Tuscumbia had received

The envelope that contained one of the letters that got Martha Cassell in trouble with Union authorities. *Fold3.com.*

a letter from a Rebel soldier with another letter enclosed for forwarding to Martha Washington in St. Louis. The letter that Martha Cassell picked up on the morning of February 6 appeared to be a similar letter, and Union authorities were waiting to arrest her almost immediately after she called at the post office.[187]

Although the content of Rogers's latest letter was fairly harmless, the simple fact that Martha had been caught corresponding with a known Rebel desperado was sufficient to warrant her arrest, and she was taken to the provost marshal general's office for interrogation. Martha said that neither she nor her sister Mary had any relations in the Confederate army. She admitted being a Southern sympathizer but stressed that Mary was not. She denied using the name "Martha Washington" to correspond with Rebel soldiers and prisoners, claiming that Martha Washington was a secessionist friend of hers who had asked her to pick up letters for her from time to time. However, she declined to say anything else about the mysterious Martha Washington. She admitted to having written letters to Southern soldiers before Union authorities placed restrictions on such activity, but she had not done so since. She then refused to answer further questions, and she was committed to the St. Charles Street Female Prison.[188]

If the several letters from Priest and the January letter from Rogers had been the only evidence against her, Martha might have gotten off easier than she did. Unfortunately for her, that proved not to be the case. At or near the time of her arrest, a U.S. policeman was ordered to search Martha's baggage. He turned up other letters that Martha had received from Southern soldiers and prisoners, including one written by Rogers in late December (likely the one that had arrived in Tuscumbia in early January). Then, a few days after Martha's arrest, one last letter from Rogers addressed to Martha Washington arrived in St. Louis. It was the most damning one yet. In it, Rogers told her about the Copperhead uprising that he'd instigated in Clark County, Illinois. The armed uprising had been quickly quashed by local furloughed Union soldiers, but Rogers was proud of his exploits nonetheless. "If there is a chance for guerrilla warfare," he said, "I am in....I want to see a Civil War and wild desolation sweep the north, I want a chance to avenge the insults and indignities heaped upon the people of Missouri."[189]

Martha remained in prison for several months with no action taken in her case. On June 8, she suffered an attack of dysentery, and three days later, D.R. Luyties, a St. Louis doctor, visited her at the prison. Luyties wrote to attorney W.A. Keyser, saying that Martha was dangerously ill. Not only did she have dysentery, but she also was consumptive and had been spitting blood. Luyties feared for her life and thought she should be paroled.[190]

On June 18, Martha appealed directly to Keyser. Not only was she dangerously ill, she said, but her jail mates Mrs. Haynes and Mrs. Wood (whose stories are chronicled in other chapters) were also quite sick, and she had been subjected to almost insufferable tyranny during her imprisonment. She and four other inmates were kept "huddled together in a close room," the atmosphere was poisonous, and they were almost entirely unattended. She requested that Keyser pay her a visit so that she could more fully explain her situation.[191]

But Keyser had already intervened on her behalf, and Provost Marshal General John Sanderson referred Martha's case to his personal physician, Dr. David Tandy, with a request that he visit the prison and report on the conditions, sanitary and otherwise, that he found there. Tandy reported back on June 20 that Miss Cassell had recently suffered from dysentery but was gradually regaining her strength. She was "of slight and delicate frame" with tuberculosis deposits on one lung, and he thought her life would be short. Dr. Tandy noted that any imprisonment was not conducive to health, as fresh air and exercise would be. He found the other prisoners in good health but thought they, like Miss Cassell, would benefit from keeping open the door to their room so that air could circulate. Tandy said he had no way of knowing whether Miss Cassell's complaint of abuse had any credence.

He could only say in that regard that the prisoners had plenty of wholesome food for dinner when he was there.[192]

Perhaps spurred by Martha's failing health and her complaint of mistreatment, Union authorities finally turned their attention to her case in earnest. On June 24, initial charges were drawn up accusing Martha of corresponding with the enemy, attempting to convey letters to the enemy, and assuming an alias for deceitful and disloyal purposes. The same day, General Rosecrans ordered that she be tried by military commission, and assistant solicitor William F. Dewey wrote to Clifford Thomas, judge advocate of the military commission, calling Thomas's attention to the letter from the desperado Rogers that was found in Martha's possession. Dewey considered Martha a "very rank rebel" who was "dangerous to be at liberty," and he thought she was no doubt guilty of much they could not prove. "She refuses to say anything," Dewey concluded, "and will not be sworn."[193]

Officially charged with "corresponding with and encouraging rebel enemies of the United States," Martha was tried on June 28, the same day as Pauline White. Martha pleaded guilty to the charge and also to the specification that she had exchanged letters with L. Rogers, "a notorious rebel enemy of the United States," who was then lurking about Clark County, Illinois, encouraging rebellion. Martha had failed to report his activities, even though she knew he was "evilly disposed" toward the United States. She was sentenced to imprisonment in the Missouri State Penitentiary for the duration of the war, but she was first returned to the female prison in St. Louis to await promulgation of the sentence.[194]

On July 17, Martha wrote to Colonel Sanderson, informing him that her health was failing rapidly and thanking him for his past kindnesses, including sending his personal physician to her. She asked that Sanderson arrange an interview for her with General Rosecrans so that she could lay her case before him. If she were released, she promised to go home, assuming she was strong enough to make it home, and to "interfere with no government under the sun." General Rosecrans replied two days later that Martha had forfeited any special consideration by her "passionate behavior" but that he would see what could be done for her.[195]

Apparently, nothing could be done.

On August 17, 1864, Martha's sentence was officially promulgated, and she and Pauline White were transferred together from St. Louis to Jefferson City on August 24. Martha's friends almost immediately began petitioning for her release. On September 3, two citizens from Palmyra wrote to President Lincoln, vouching for Martha's good character."[196]

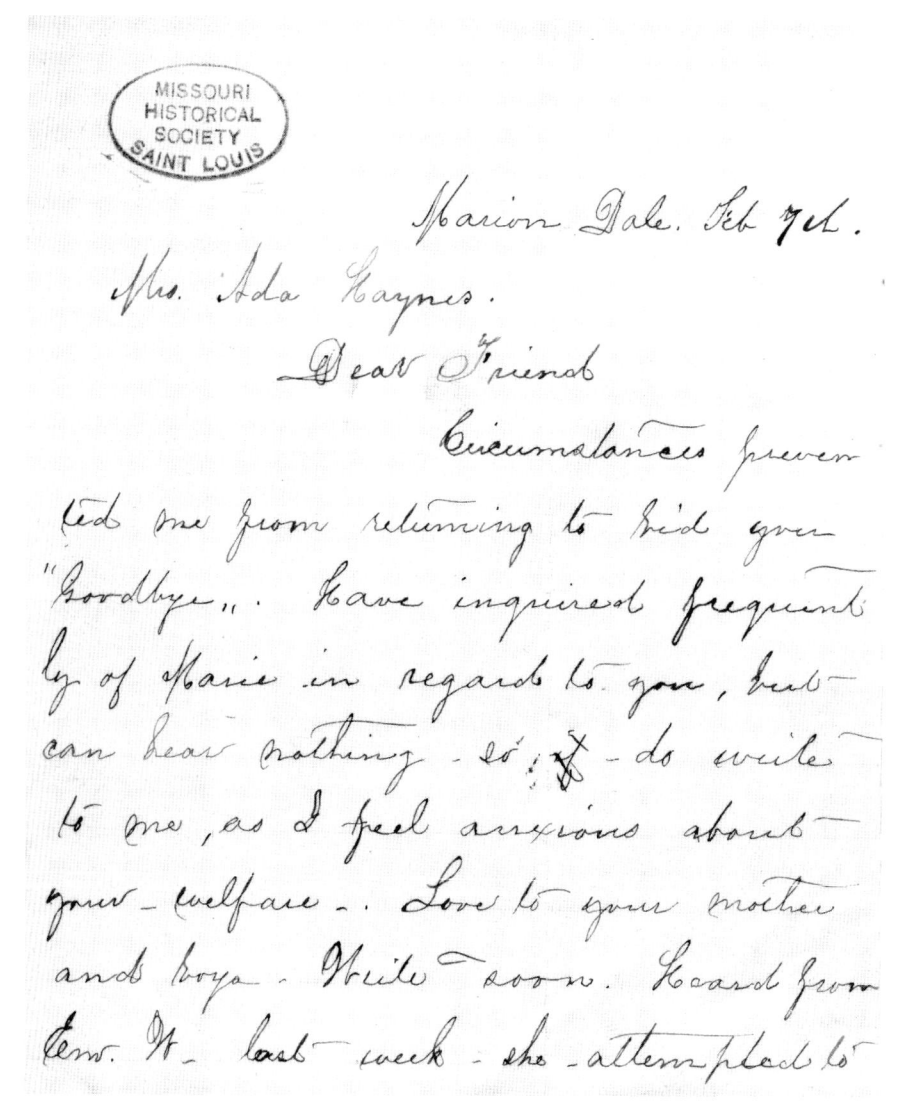

Martha Cassell letter to Addie Haynes, dated February 7 (1865), after Martha was released from prison and Addie was still in exile in New York City. *Missouri Historical Society, St. Louis.*

On September 17, Martha gave a statement at the penitentiary no doubt meant to bolster the argument of those pleading for the mitigation of her sentence. She said she had corresponded with Lewis Rogers only to be cordial, not with the intention of giving aid and comfort to the enemy. She admitted that she sympathized with the South, but she never intended to be treasonous and was not trying to aid the rebellion. She also pointed out that she had never received Rogers's last letter, which was the most damning evidence presented at her trial, and that she had not replied to the previous one.[197]

Influential allies, including Missouri Supreme Court justice John D.S. Dryden, soon got involved in Martha's case. In late October, Dryden wrote to Edward Bates, President Lincoln's attorney general, describing Martha as "a young lady of unspotted reputation, intelligent and refined, quiet and modest in her behavior, of a sensitive and generous nature, possessing an exceedingly frail constitution." Although her offense was a "grave indiscretion," Dryden thought she had committed it "without criminal intent."[198]

Lincoln pardoned Martha on October 25, and she was discharged from the penitentiary on October 31 (while Pauline White would wait another eight months for her release). On February 7, 1865, Martha wrote to her old cellmate Ada Haynes expressing her concern for the older woman's welfare, but it's not clear where she was when she penned the letter. After the war, though, she went home to Marion County, where she married Washington West in 1868. She apparently died, or else they separated shortly afterward, since her husband was back home living with his parents two years later.[199]

12

A Guileless Escapade

Missouri Wood Buys Her Way Out of Prison

Union justice in Civil War Missouri wasn't always blind. Pretty or charming women sometimes received preferential treatment. So, too, did women from well-to-do or prominent families. Perhaps in no case was a woman's wealth more influential in winning her freedom than that of Mrs. Missouri Wood, who simply bought her way out of prison.

The daughter of Solomon P. Ketchum, a former St. Louis city assessor and recorder, Missouri was born about 1826 in Missouri. In 1851, she married Edward Wood, and in 1860, she and her husband were living in St. Louis in the Seventh Ward with two of her siblings, her mother, and an adopted child. Shortly after this, she and Edward had a child of their own.[200]

Missouri came to the attention of Union authority in late February 1864 for helping her friend Mary Doyle, an accused Rebel spy, get out of St. Louis undetected. The previous summer, Mrs. Doyle had gone south at her own request with a group of banished St. Louis citizens in order to be near her husband, a soldier in the Confederate army. She'd returned to St. Louis without a pass in early February and, under the name of Mrs. Harrison, stayed initially with the Southern-sympathizing family of Sarah McCammot. Mary's four sisters, who also lived in the city, did not share her political sentiments, but after a few days, she went to stay with one of them, Lizzie Cottrill. Somewhere along the line, Mary and Missouri, who had known each other since before the war, also reunited.[201]

Union authorities somehow learned of Mary Doyle's presence in the city, but before they could locate and arrest her, she left St. Louis on February

17 aboard the steamboat *Mary E. Forsythe* headed back to the South. On Saturday, February 20, Union authorities questioned a number of people, including three of Mary's sisters, from whom they learned that Missouri Wood had helped procure Mary's passage through her acquaintance with the boat clerk, John Sites. When Missouri was arrested later the same day, she denied even knowing Mary Doyle, her sisters, or anyone on the steamboat *Mary E. Forsythe*. She suggested she was a victim of mistaken identity, and she was released after questioning. Now that she was under suspicion from Federal authorities, though, she knew she had to do something about the stash of money she had hidden at her house. It amounted to over $5,000, money her husband had given her for safekeeping a couple of weeks earlier before leaving St. Louis for New Orleans. She decided to deposit the cash in a bank, but on Monday morning Missouri was re-arrested at her home just as she was getting ready to start downtown with the money. She had it in her pocket as she was taken to the police office for additional questioning. She again denied any knowledge of Mary Doyle, but Mary's sisters, brought to the office for reexamination, confirmed that Missouri was the same woman who had helped Mary leave St. Louis. Missouri was officially charged with harboring a spy, and she was taken under guard to an unspecified place of detention. During the trip, she mentioned to the officer escorting her that she had some money and asked whether she could take it with her. Without asking the amount, he replied that she could, and she didn't tell him the amount. Little did the officer know that she was carrying $5,300, a small fortune in 1864![202]

Once inside the lockup, Missouri waited until she was alone that evening. She then took the money from her pocket and tucked it into the folds of her skirt. A few weeks later, Missouri was transferred to the St. Charles Street Female Military Prison.[203]

In March 1864, Colonel Sanderson launched an investigation into the Order of American Knights and other secret societies working against the Union in Missouri. Both Missouri Wood and Martha Cassell (see chapter 11) merited particular mention in his June 12 report to General Rosecrans detailing the investigation. The work of the secret societies was facilitated

Missouri Wood. *Missouri Historical Society, St. Louis.*

On the day Missouri Wood was arrested, Union authorities searched her home similar to the way the soldiers are searching the home in this sketch. *Library of Congress.*

by an organized network of Rebel mail handlers, and Missouri and Martha were among a number of sophisticated young women "engaged in the treasonable work of receiving and forwarding these mails."[204]

The file containing the statements authorities had gathered in February to be used as evidence against Missouri was misplaced or removed on purpose by some unknown party before she could come to trial, thereby delaying the proceeding. In late July 1864, when the trial had still not been scheduled, Sarah Ketchum, Missouri's mother, wrote to General Rosecrans, pleading for him to do whatever he could to hasten the trial date. Sarah said she was an old woman who depended on her daughter for support. She'd been forced to take care of Missouri's child for the past five months, but her advanced age and a recent attack of rheumatism made it impossible for her to continue much longer. Sarah also asked for leniency for Missouri. She assured Rosecrans that Missouri would willingly take an oath of allegiance and give bonds, and she blamed her daughter's current trouble on the fact that she was "not a woman of strong mind" and had always been "easily imposed upon." In her youth, Missouri was "perfectly childish," Sarah said, and Sarah and her husband often worried that they might have to commit her to an insane asylum. Missouri had since been restored to health, but she was still a fragile personality, according to her mother.[205]

Shortly after Mrs. Ketchum's letter to Rosecrans, the provost marshal general's office began reexamining some of the same witnesses who had been interviewed in Missouri's case back in February. Lizzie Cottrill, who lived near Missouri Wood, said she didn't know whether her sister Mary had brought any letters to St. Louis in early 1864, when she arrived from the South. Lizzie said Mary was at her house as she prepared to return to the South and that Missouri was there, too. Lizzie heard Mrs. Wood tell Mary that she had arranged for a young woman named Nellie Scott to procure Mary's passage.[206]

General William Rosecrans, who entertained the entreaties of Sarah Ketchum on behalf of her daughter Missouri Wood. *Missouri Historical Society, St. Louis.*

When Missouri Wood was examined on August 24, four days after Lizzie, she still denied even knowing Mary Doyle or any of her sisters. After the examiner supplied Lizzie Cottrill's address, Missouri insisted that she'd never visited anyone at that address. She had never received mail from anyone coming from the South, and, furthermore, she didn't even know anyone who had come to St. Louis from the South except people she'd met in prison. She didn't know Nellie Scott, didn't know the boat clerk Sites, and didn't know anyone who'd ever carried Rebel letters. She did not sympathize with the South, and she sincerely wished to see the authority of the United States restored over the whole country.[207]

Because Missouri's denials directly contradicted the sisters' statements, Union authorities sought to strengthen their case against her by examining additional witnesses. John E. Sites, the *Mary E. Forsythe* clerk, was interviewed on September 10. Sites, who'd been arrested about the same time as Missouri Wood and released on parole, said he'd been introduced to Mrs. Wood in mid-1863, and he remembered her coming to the boat in January or February 1864. Neither she nor Miss Nellie Scott, however, ever negotiated with him concerning anyone's passage on the boat, and he did not know Mary Doyle.[208]

Interviewed on September 17, Nellie Scott said she'd met Missouri Wood going to Memphis on the *Mary E. Forsythe* in 1863 and introduced her to Sites but that she didn't know Mary Doyle or her sisters. Nellie admitted she'd helped secure passage for certain people, but she had not done so for Mrs. Wood. Re-interviewed two days later, Nellie had gotten over her temporary amnesia. She clarified that she had, indeed, accompanied Mrs. Wood to the *Mary E. Forsythe* on February 15 or 16, 1864, and talked to John Sites on Mrs. Wood's behalf about securing passage for a friend of hers who wanted to go south to reunite with her children and didn't have the means to pay her way. Nellie said she did not know the name of Mrs. Wood's friend and that she acted only out of charity.[209]

Meanwhile, Missouri Wood was tiring of life inside the St. Charles Street Female Prison, and she decided to leverage her wealth to try to gain her freedom. Around the first of September, she'd watched another young woman, Elizabeth Newcomer, escape. As soon as Elizabeth was outside, Missouri had tossed her bonnet out a window for the woman to don so she wouldn't attract attention and be recognized because of her uncovered head. Missouri thought the prison keeper, William Dickson, should have seen Mrs. Newcomer's escape if he'd been alert. Based on conversations she'd overheard between Dickson and members of his family, Missouri suspected he was corrupt and might even have been in on the escape. Although Dickson didn't know Missouri had a slew of money on her person, he knew she was wealthy, because her husband had sent word that he would pay any amount necessary to get her out on bail. In early September, according to Missouri's later story, Dickson told her, in an apparent effort to extort money from her, that he thought she would probably be shot or else spend the duration of the war in prison. Missouri responded that she could get money if he thought it might help in winning her release. Dickson said he would "see about it" but that it would probably cost $4,000 for him to go through the legal channels to get her released. Missouri promptly produced the $4,000, but a week or so later, when she asked him about his effort to get her released, he told her that it was unsuccessful. If she could come up with another $1,000, however, he might find a more direct way for her to get her freedom. On the evening of September 24, he slipped her a key, and she handed over the additional $1,000. Using the key, Missouri let herself and fellow inmate Emily Weaver out an alley door of the prison early the next morning, just after the overnight guards had gone off duty. Hastily making her way through the streets, Mrs. Wood immediately crossed the Mississippi River into Illinois and started north, not tarrying to try to see her loved ones. She made her way to Chicago and, after staying there a day or so, reached Windsor, Canada, four days after her escape.[210]

On reaching Windsor on September 29, Missouri immediately wrote a letter to her sister, letting her know where she was and explaining how she had escaped. She said that once outside the prison, she had changed bonnets, put on an old shawl, and donned spectacles, which "made my disguise complete." Missouri told her sister she would love to see her and the rest of the family but probably would never be able to do so while the war continued.[211]

Missouri's letter to her sister somehow fell into the hands of Union authorities. Shortly after her escape, two other young women had escaped from the St. Charles Street Female Prison, and on October 21, Provost Marshal General Darr shut the place down because of the recent rash of breakouts. William Dickson's wife had given a statement the day after Wood's escape denying any knowledge of how she and Miss Weaver obtained the key except to suggest that Miss Weaver's father might have slipped it to them during a visit the day before. But Darr suspected the prison keeper was at least guilty of negligence and might even have been complicit in one or more of the recent escapes. Continuing the investigation into the activities of the Order of American Knights and other disloyal elements in Missouri begun by his predecessor, Darr wrote to Wood in Canada on November 16, asking her if she would be willing to inform him of the circumstances surrounding her escape. She replied on November 25 that she was quite willing to cooperate if Darr would give his assurance that her family would be protected from reprisal by those whom she might implicate.[212]

Given the necessary assurance, Mrs. Wood gave a statement on December 12 accusing Dickson of abusing her and some of the other prisoners under his watch, and she detailed the bribes she had paid him to gain her release. She also implicated Lieutenant Isaac C. Dodge, an assistant in the provost marshal general's office, in the scheme. Based on Missouri's statement and other evidence, Darr had Dickson arrested, but he was immediately released on parole under bond and was ultimately not prosecuted for any alleged wrongdoing, even though Missouri gave another statement on December 22 further implicating him in corrupt practices at the prison. In her later statement, Missouri also added that Lieutenant Dodge often visited the prison and spent an inordinate amount of time alone with Miss Weaver. She said she noticed this in particular because she knew Dodge had a family in the city. Missouri said she escaped because of the deplorable conditions in the prison and because she despaired of her case ever coming to trial, not because she was guilty of any wrongdoing. She claimed not even to know why she'd been arrested.[213]

Although several of the women who'd previously sworn to Missouri Wood's involvement in procuring passage south for Mary Doyle gave additional statements after her escape reiterating her participation, it hardly mattered, since Missouri remained out of reach of Union military authority. She returned to Missouri after the war and was living in St. Louis in 1870 with her husband, son, and adopted daughter. Her father, Solomon Ketchum, died in 1877, leaving almost everything to his second wife and their children. The following year, Missouri and her siblings by his first wife unsuccessfully contested the will.[214]

Missouri and her husband moved to Colorado before 1880. She died there in 1894 and was brought back to Missouri for burial in St. Louis's Bellefontaine Cemetery.[215]

13

Emily Weaver

Sentenced to Hang Higher than Haman

The story of Emily Weaver, the young woman who escaped from the St. Charles Street Female Prison with Missouri Wood, is even more intriguing than Wood's. Only seventeen years old, Weaver was convicted of being a Confederate spy and sentenced to hang. The guilty verdict was based largely on the testimony of a jailhouse snitch, and Emily's escapade with Wood had nothing to do with the severity of her punishment. Fortunately for Emily, General Rosecrans decided that the testimony of a single, dubious witness was scant evidence on which to send a teenage girl to the gallows. He disapproved her sentence, thus reserving the dishonor of being the first female executed by the U.S. government to Mary Surratt, convicted as a conspirator in the assassination of President Lincoln less than a year later.

The only girl in a family of eight children, Emily was born in Pennsylvania about 1847 to Abram and Mary Weaver. The family lived in Philadelphia, where Abram Weaver practiced law. Around the fall of 1860, Mrs. Weaver, a Virginia native and Southern sympathizer, moved with her kids to Batesville, Arkansas, where her sister Nancy Burr already lived. Mr. Weaver stayed behind in Philadelphia to attend to business, and when the Civil War came on, he joined the Union army. Meanwhile, at least three of his sons in Arkansas joined the Rebel army, and Abram did not reunite with the rest of the family as planned, making it only as far as Memphis.[216]

In the fall of 1862, twenty-two-year-old Wilson L. Tilley, a former Rebel soldier, came to Batesville from Pulaski County, Missouri, took up residence there, and made Emily's acquaintance. When the Federals later occupied

Batesville, they contracted with Tilley to buy horses and mules for them, and Emily was also on friendly terms with many of the Federal officers, sometimes entertaining them in the Weaver home. Despite their familiarity with Union soldiers, both Emily and Tilley had dubious reputations for loyalty. Tilley had taken the oath of allegiance three times since he'd left Confederate service, but the fact that once wasn't enough only added to some people's doubts about him. Since coming to Batesville, he'd made at least one known trip to a Rebel camp accompanying the wife of a Confederate officer, and it was suspected that he frequently went back and forth between Rebel and Federal lines.[217]

In the spring of 1864, the Federals abandoned Batesville, and part of Confederate general Joseph Orville "Jo" Shelby's command occupied the place on May 26. Later the same day, Emily wrote to Tilley, postponing a trip they had been planning to start on the twenty-seventh. "It would not look right for us to go right off just when 'our men' have arrived," she said. "It would look like we wanted to avoid them, and God knows I am too overjoyed to see them for that." She told Tilley to feel free to go on without her, however, if he still wanted to leave the next day as planned. Except for the fondness she expressed for Southern soldiers, the letter contained little that could be construed as incriminating, but Emily cautioned Tilley not to show the letter to anyone and to keep quiet about their proposed trip, as they might "get off all right yet."[218]

After General Shelby arrived in Batesville on May 28, Emily quickly had a change of heart about postponing her trip. On May 29, she, her cousin Charles Burr, and Tilley's acquaintance Eleanor King left Batesville on horseback headed for Missouri, escorted by Burr's father, Edwin. The next day, a few miles north of Batesville, they rendezvoused with Tilley, who had left town on the twenty-eighth to avoid conscription into Shelby's army, and Edwin Burr returned to Batesville. His fifteen-year-old son was going east to go to school, and Mrs. King, whose husband had died during Confederate service, was returning to her home at Rolla, Missouri. Emily was going to Memphis to see her father, and Tilley had promised to accompany the ladies and the young boy.[219]

Several days out from Batesville, the party of four was intercepted in southern Missouri by some men belonging to Colonel Timothy Reeves's irregular Confederate force. Despite Tilley showing the men a Confederate pass, the guerrillas stole his and Burr's horses, leaving one old nag in exchange. The foursome then made their way to Pilot Knob, where they shipped the remaining horses to St. Louis for sale.[220]

Left: Emily Weaver is shown a few years after the war. *From the* Independence County (AR) Chronicle.

Right: General Joseph "Jo" Shelby, for whom Emily Weaver allegedly spied. *Author's collection.*

Taking a train, the group reached St. Louis on June 6 and stopped at the Lindell Hotel. The next day, Eleanor went to the home of Mary Jane Lingow in Carondelet, a St. Louis suburb, while Tilley and Emily tarried in St. Louis. They joined Eleanor at the Lingow place on or about June 8, and Emily's cousin Charles Burr resumed his journey east about the same time. Both Tilley and Eleanor knew Mary Jane and her daughters Sue and Laura Belle, because the Lingow family had lived in Pulaski County until the fall of 1862. Tilley and Belle had been romantically involved at one point.[221]

After spending the night at the Lingow place, Emily, Eleanor, Belle, and Tilley went back to St. Louis and stopped at the Wedge House, a hotel or boardinghouse run by one of Tilley's former teachers. Tilley promptly left for Illinois to see a man who owed him money, while Emily, Eleanor, and Belle stayed one night at the Wedge House. The next day, Eleanor took a train to Rolla, and Emily accompanied her. Emily remained in Rolla two days and two nights and then came back to the Lingow home at Carondelet. Returning from Illinois, Tilley met her there the next day, and he and Emily went back to St. Louis. They stayed in the city two or three days, and Captain H.H. Ribble, a Union officer who'd known them in Batesville, saw them on the streets. Knowing their reputation for disloyalty, he wondered why they were in St. Louis. He reported his suspicions to Union authorities, and U.S. detectives were detailed to watch the pair. After a couple of days in St. Louis, Tilley left for Illinois again, because he'd been unable to finish his business during his previous trip, and Emily went back to Carondelet to stay with the Lingow family. On Sunday, June 19, she wrote a letter to Eleanor saying that she would be leaving Mrs. Lingow's by the middle of the coming week and that she would then "fulfill [her] promise."[222]

On or about June 20, Belle Lingow told Emily that a woman wanted to see her at the home of a neighbor, Mrs. Eliza Bull. At Bull's place, another woman, Mary Rayburn, told Emily that she (Emily) was being watched by U.S. detectives and warned her against doing anything that could get the Lingow family in trouble. According to Rayburn's later testimony, Emily grew indignant at the suggestion that she might be engaged in disloyal activities.[223]

Emily's arrest came sooner than either she or Ms. Rayburn might have guessed. The very next day, Tilley, having returned from Illinois, showed up at the Lingow place, and just a few minutes after his arrival, detectives came to take him and Emily into Federal custody. In addition, the detectives confiscated a number of letters, and the Confederate pass under which Emily and Tilley had left Arkansas was also found, either at the time of their arrest or shortly afterward. The two prisoners were escorted to St. Louis, where Tilley was lodged in the Myrtle Street Prison and Emily in the St. Charles Street Female Prison.[224]

Emily's movements alone over the previous three weeks were enough to bring suspicion on her. If she was going to see her father as she said, why had she come 180 miles overland to Pilot Knob, where she still faced a train ride to St. Louis and a long steamboat trip downriver to Memphis, rather than travel 120 miles east-southeast directly to Memphis? Why, too, had she gone back to Rolla after reaching St. Louis?[225]

The letters seized at the Lingow home and in Eleanor King's possession when she, too, was arrested in Rolla on June 22 only added to the Federals' suspicion. References to Rebel soldiers as "our boys" and similar allusions made it clear that Emily and the people with whom she'd recently been associating harbored Southern sympathies. And what did she mean by telling Eleanor, after visiting Rolla, that she would soon be leaving St. Louis to fulfill her promise?[226]

Early in the war, this slave pen at the corner of Fifth and Myrtle in St. Louis was converted to Myrtle Street Prison, where's Emily's sidekick, Lee Tilley, was confined. *Missouri Historical Society, St. Louis.*

But Emily had a logical explanation for most of the seemingly incriminating circumstances. She'd come the circuitous route so that she would have the safety of company and because the roads between Batesville and Memphis were swampy and almost impassable. She'd gone to Rolla to visit Tilley's relatives so that she would have something to do while he was in Illinois and so that she could see more of the country. The Confederate pass was not hers. Eleanor King had procured it.[227]

Therefore, the evidence gathered so far, even taken together, fell well short of proving what Union authorities suspected—namely, that Emily Weaver was a Confederate spy. So they set about solidifying their case by taking statements from Emily, her recent associates, and Union soldiers who'd known her in Batesville.

Examined on June 24, Emily said she'd taken the oath of allegiance in Memphis the previous September and that the only time she'd been inside Rebel lines since then was when General Shelby came to Batesville just before she left for St. Louis. She had brought no contraband from Batesville, only personal items such as clothing. Emily said she knew nothing firsthand about the loyalty of the Lingow women but had heard they were Southern sympathizers. Emily may have lost some credibility when she added that she thought Eleanor King was a loyal woman, because her examiner knew or would soon learn that Mrs. King was a professed Southern sympathizer. Emily said her father was a commission merchant in Memphis and her cousin was on his way to New York to attend school.[228]

Mary Jane Lingow was interviewed on June 24, the same day as Emily, and Laura Belle Lingow on June 25. Both women were very reluctant to say anything damaging against Emily. In fact, the U.S. detective who arrested Mrs. Lingow reported that she told him that no punishment could induce her to tell what went on at Mrs. Bull's house. Only toward the end of lengthy interrogations did Mary Jane and her daughter finally admit that they themselves were Southern sympathizers and that Emily probably was, too, but they denied anything more incriminating than that.[229]

Interrogated some days later, Tilley spent most of the interview defending his own movements and activities, but when asked about Miss Weaver, he said he thought she was probably a Confederate sympathizer. He'd never heard of her going into Confederate territory, however, and he confirmed that going to Memphis to visit her father was her purpose in coming into Missouri.[230]

James Shepherd, a Union soldier who'd been stationed at Batesville, said Emily had the reputation of being a Southern sympathizer, but he thought she was "a very truthful girl." He'd never heard of her going into Rebel lines and didn't believe she was a Rebel mail carrier.[231]

To the contrary, Captain Ribble, the officer who'd sicced the Union authorities on Emily in the first place, said she had a reputation of going back and forth between Rebel and Federal camps. Ribble added that Emily "made herself very familiar" with Union soldiers, and he thought it was for the purpose of "obtaining information from them that might be useful to the Rebels."[232]

Emily gave another statement on July 7, justifying and explaining in more detail her movements from the time she left Batesville until she was arrested. She added that another reason she had come by way of St. Louis rather than going the more direct route to Memphis was to accompany her young cousin.[233]

On July 14, Emily wrote to Colonel Sanderson, urging him to attend to her case. "I solemnly assure you, sir, that my present visit was made with not the remotest idea of engaging in politics, or in war matters generally." She said she'd been contemplating a trip to Memphis for some time to see her father and was eager to resume the journey. The fact that Union officers in Batesville knew of her plan, she told Sanderson, proved that the visit to her father was not a recently hatched scheme, "as some seem to think." She said that, if she'd done anything wrong, it was purely unintentional, and she reiterated her desire that Sanderson see to her case, even if it meant she would be banished.[234]

Thus far, there was virtually no solid evidence against Emily, and Sanderson might have acted on her request had not Mary Ann Pitman entered the picture. On July 16, Pitman, a fellow inmate at the St. Charles Street Prison, gave by far the most damning statement against Emily. Early in the war, Pitman had disguised herself as a man and served in the Confederate army. Later, after revealing her true gender, she worked as a Confederate spy, making multiple trips to St. Louis in that capacity. Captured by Federal forces in the spring of 1864, she said that even before she was captured she'd begun to have a change of heart and that she now felt the Union was in the right. She reached a tacit agreement with Colonel Sanderson that if she would help in his campaign to root out secret Confederate societies like the Order of the American Knights and perform other spy missions, he would advocate for leniency in her case. Not long before Emily's arrest, Pitman, a woman of numerous aliases, was placed in the St. Charles Street Female Prison under the name of Molly Hayes to investigate rumored corruption at the facility and to gather intelligence from her fellow prisoners. When Emily was arrested, she was placed in Pitman's room on direct orders from Sanderson.[235]

Pitman recalled that on the night Emily came to the prison, she (Pitman) pretended to be a strong Confederate sympathizer in order to gain Emily's trust, and she exclaimed how awful the "wretched Yankees" were to imprison women. Finally, she asked Emily what she had done to warrant imprisonment, and Emily said she'd done a lot. However, she (Emily) didn't think the Federals knew very much about it, and she thought she'd soon be released, partly because she'd won favor with Lieutenant Dodge of the provost marshal general's office. Dodge thought she was "too good looking and had too innocent a face" to be kept in prison. Emily said she'd take the oath a dozen times if the Federals wanted her to in order to be released, because the oath didn't mean anything to her.[236]

Emily gradually opened up and started telling "Molly" the specifics of what she'd done for the Confederacy. She said she'd been in Confederate service as a spy for almost two years and had even been made an honorary colonel. She would go inside enemy lines to learn the layout of Union fortifications, the number of Federal soldiers, and the quality and quantity of their arms, and she would report back to the Rebels. She earned seventy-five dollars a month for such work.

Emily said she and Tilley, who was also a spy, had been sent into Missouri by General Shelby, who came to Emily's house on the night she left on her mission. They'd gathered intelligence about Federal military preparedness at Pilot Knob, St. Louis, and Rolla. The report that she planned to deliver to Shelby was hidden at the Lingow home.[237]

Emily was afraid that, if she was kept very long, the Federals would find enough evidence against her to "hang her higher than Haman a dozen times." She showed Pitman a small pistol she had concealed on her person, and she said that, if she wasn't released soon, she'd get out one way or another even if she had "to shoot her way out." Afraid of being caught with the incriminating pistol, Emily gave it to Pitman and asked her to hide it. Instead of concealing it, Pittman turned it over to authorities and told Emily, when she asked about it, that it had been stolen. Emily also had in her possession a pair of buckskin gloves with the inscription "Col. E.H. Weaver, C.S.A." written on them. Since they were even more incriminating than the pistol, Emily cut them up and tried to burn them at the prison, but Pitman later sent for Lieutenant Dodge, who retrieved the remnants of the gloves from the fireplace as evidence.[238]

While Pitman thought Emily was certainly a spy, she did not believe the girl was a member of the Order of American Knights, since she did not know the secret signs that Pitman flashed.[239]

On July 21, having heard rumors that someone had brought serious allegations against her, Emily again wrote to Sanderson. She assured the colonel that such allegations were false and that whoever had leveled them had "perjured himself in the sight of God and man." Emily said she was totally innocent, and she again asked that Sanderson attend to her case promptly.[240]

Emily had written to her father shortly after her imprisonment, and on July 25, Edwin Burr, who'd learned of his niece's predicament through Mr. Weaver, arrived in St. Louis. He engaged Colonel James O. Broadhead, former provost marshal general, as Emily's lawyer and began working on his own for her release.[241]

Arraigned for trial by military commission on August 2, Emily was charged with being a spy and with violating the laws of war by coming within Federal lines and lurking about Missouri, under the pretense of visiting her father in Memphis, for the purpose of obtaining military information for the Rebel enemies of the United States. Specifically, she had spied on Union forces at Pilot Knob and St. Louis. Emily pleaded not guilty to both charges and to the specifications. The *St. Louis Daily Missouri Democrat* called Emily at the time of her arraignment "a deceiver of the gayest kind."[242]

At trial in early August, Mary Ann Pitman was the star prosecution witness. She testified largely to the same facts she'd related in her earlier statement. Most of the other witnesses also echoed what they'd said earlier. Major William McClellan, a Union officer who had not previously been deposed, testified for the defense that he had given Emily the buckskin gloves at Batesville as a joke.[243]

Colonel Broadhead's closing statement in Emily's defense attacked two of the prosecution witnesses in particular: Frank Riley, the detective who'd arrested her; and Mary Pitman, the jailhouse snitch. According to the defense, Riley thought everything Emily did was suspicious simply because he'd been placed on assignment specifically to watch her. Broadhead blamed Emily's arrest, which never should have happened, on "the imagination of a stupid detective." The colonel attacked Mary Pitman in even harsher terms. She was "an artful and deceiving woman" and "a traitor of the worst type" whose testimony was "unworthy of credit" because she had fabricated it in the hope of gaining favor with Union authorities in order "to save herself from the gallows." Even in the unlikely event that some of Pitman's testimony was true, it was understandable that a young Southern woman might invent or exaggerate stories to try to impress an older woman she thought to be a Confederate spy. Broadhead also sought to refute much of the evidence against Emily that had been presented in the case, such as her burning of the gloves inscribed with her name and her supposed rank in the Confederate army. Even though a Federal officer, Major McClellan, had written the inscription as a joke, Emily knew the gloves might be construed as evidence against her. In fact, Broadhead pointed out, the Federal officers who knew Emily best, such as McClellan, considered her an honorable and upstanding young woman.[244]

In refuting the defense's statement, the judge advocate for the prosecution reiterated the evidence against Emily, including her suspicious movements. He also said Ms. Pitman's testimony was given naturally with no hint of duplicity. He admitted she had been a spy, but she had given herself up voluntarily. And the only reason the Federal officers in Batesville found Miss Weaver to be such an upstanding and nice young lady, the judge advocate suggested, was that she was deliberately deceiving them in order to gain information.[245]

On August 9, Emily was found guilty and sentenced "to be hanged by the neck until she is dead at such time and place as the Commanding General may direct." On August 27, Brigadier General Thomas Ewing Jr., commanding the District of St. Louis, approved the proceedings but with a recommendation to General Rosecrans that the verdict be mitigated. However, Rosecrans did not immediately act on the case, and Edwin Burr continued proclaiming Emily's innocence and trying to gain clemency for her. Emily's father, Abram Weaver, arrived in St. Louis on September 11 to help in the effort. His main focus was trying to destroy Mary Ann Pitman's credibility, and he began gathering evidence of her alleged unsavory character. On September 23, U.S. Chief of Detectives Peter Tallon reported Weaver's activities to Sanderson, suggesting that any incriminating evidence or testimony against Ms. Pitman that Weaver might come up with should have been presented at trial.[246]

Additional statements, both for and against Emily, were gathered from late August into the latter part of September, long after the trial had concluded. One of those giving a deposition in Emily's favor was Elisha Baxter, who was her next-door neighbor in Batesville and a U.S. senator from Arkansas in the state's reconstituted Federal government. Although the report to General Shelby that Emily had supposedly hidden at the Lingow home never turned up, the favorable statements on her behalf were offset by the testimony of two Black residents of Batesville. One man swore that Emily and her whole family in Batesville were "nothing but secesh" and that he'd heard her "extoll Jeff Davis to the skies."[247]

While opposing forces continued to spar over the question of Emily Weaver's guilt, something happened in late September that upset the proverbial apple cart even more. Emily, following Missouri Wood's lead, escaped from the St. Charles Street Prison on the morning of September 25.[248]

In response to the escape, Colonel Sanderson threatened punishment to anyone who aided the fugitives in their flight, and several Southern sympathizers, including Emily's father and uncle, were arrested as hostages for their return. Wood, of course, made a beeline for Canada and did not return to Missouri during the war. However, Emily apparently did not accompany her. Mrs. Wood gave no indication in her letters to Colonel Darr that such was the case, and Martha Cassell said in her February 1865 letter to Addie Haynes that Emily had recently tried to come up the river to St. Louis but had not been able to go beyond Cairo, Illinois, because of the ice.

This suggests that, instead of fleeing to Canada with Missouri Wood, Emily likely made her way back to Arkansas after her escape.[249]

At any rate, the verdict condemning Emily to death was finally promulgated in her absence in early November, but General Rosecrans immediately disapproved the proceedings. "The evidence of the guilt of the accused is not sufficiently conclusive," he declared. "The prisoner will be released from prison under the direction of the Provost Marshal General."[250]

Except for Mary Ann Pitman's statement, the evidence against Tilley to sustain a charge of spying was at least as strong as that against Emily, but he, unlike her, was charged only with violating his oath of allegiance and being a guerrilla/marauder acting in concert with the Rebel enemies of the Federal government. In early 1865, he was convicted on the second charge and sentenced to imprisonment for the duration of the war.[251]

At or near the close of the war, Emily returned to Batesville. She married Isaac Newton Reed on December 20, 1866. The couple had twelve children and continued to make their home in Batesville. Emily died in August 1917 and was buried at Oaklawn Cemetery in Batesville.[252]

14

SUCH A PRETTY YOUNG LADY

The Story of Jane Hancock

S aying that the Civil War often pitted neighbor against neighbor has become a cliché, but the statement's frequent use makes it no less true. It applies especially to Missouri, a border state that was occupied by the Union throughout most of the war but where Southern sympathies remained strong, particularly in the rural areas. Not only did people clash over divergent political opinions, but they sometimes also used the war as an excuse to discharge personal grudges. That may have been what happened in the case of Jane Hancock of Mississippi County.

Jane was born about 1842 in Henderson County, Kentucky, to Henderson and Rebecca (Quinn) Hancock. The family came to Missouri after 1850, and in 1860, Jane was living with her father and five siblings in Twapitty Township in Mississippi County, the mother apparently having died. Their home was located about a mile from the Mississippi River opposite Cairo, Illinois.[253]

One of Jane's friends, or at least acquaintances, was Mary "Polly" Ann Bryant, a young woman Jane's own age who lived near the Hancocks. However, on August 18, 1864, Polly Ann appeared at the Union post in Charleston, the seat of Mississippi County, to give a statement against Jane. Exactly what caused Polly Ann to turn against her friend is not clear, but she told Assistant Provost Marshal James A. Reid that she had been at Jane's home about a year earlier, during the month of August 1863, when Jane came home from Cairo. Mr. Hancock asked his daughter whether she had gotten the caps and powder, and she replied that she had about a gross of caps and four pounds of powder. Jane's clothes were muddy from riding horseback, and her father told her she should change.[254]

Polly Ann accompanied Jane into the bedroom and saw her undress. Miss Bryant complimented her friend on her "fine bustle," and Jane said, yes, it was "a very handsome one." As Jane continued to undress, Polly Ann saw a piece of calico fastened around Jane's waist containing percussion caps and four calico sacks fastened to her hoops containing gunpowder. Polly Ann asked whom they were for, and Jane replied that they were for her sweetheart, James Fugate, and another friend. She cautioned Polly Ann not to tell anyone or she would know who did. Miss Bryant kept her peace for a year, but now she'd decided to tell what she knew.[255]

The thirty-one-year-old Fugate, a suspected bushwhacker and the father of three small children, was on parole after a previous run-in with Union authorities. After Miss Bryant's statement, he was ordered to report to Charleston on August 24, 1864, and a warrant for his arrest for violating the parole was issued when he failed to appear. He showed up a few days later and claimed he hadn't reported on time because he'd been sick in Illinois. About the same time of Fugate's arrest, Mississippi County resident Henry Deal gave a statement accusing Fugate of smuggling whiskey and other items to the Rebels in the spring of 1863. Deal thought Fugate had "been at it" throughout most of the war except "when he was in the guardhouse." Fugate's case was complicated, however, by the fact that, while on parole, he had joined the Union army, and authorities didn't know whether to consider him a prisoner or an enlisted man.[256]

On August 28, Jane was arrested at the home of a neighbor and brought to the Union post at Charleston. Charged with smuggling, she was taken the next day before Lieutenant Reid, the assistant provost marshal, to whom she "most positively" denied the charge. Reid decided to forward both her and Fugate to St. Louis—Jane for trial and Fugate so that authorities there could figure out what to do with him. The prisoners were sent to St. Louis under separate escort on August 31.[257]

On reaching St. Louis, Jane was committed to Gratiot Street Prison on the evening of September 1. Griffin Frost, held prisoner at the same location, noted her arrival in his journal, saying, "She is rather good looking, and seems to be intelligent." Frost heard the Black man who cooked for the prison officers say about Jane, "When they get to be putting such pretty young ladies as she in prison, they must be nearly played out."[258]

When she first arrived at the prison, Jane was placed in the "round room" with one other female prisoner. This was a room near the center and on the

Gratiot Street Prison, where Jane Hancock was imprisoned during September 1864, as it appeared shortly after the war. *Missouri Historical Society, St. Louis.*

bottom floor of the building, half underground. The next day, when eleven other female prisoners arrived, all thirteen were taken to a larger area, what Frost called "the feminine mess."[259]

Jane was interrogated on September 2, the day after she was committed to the prison. After describing the circumstances of her arrest, she said, in response to her examiner, that she made a living by staying with relatives and doing washing and cooking. How often did she go to Cairo? About five or six times a month, she said. When she went, she usually took produce or other items to sell and usually sold five to fifteen dollars' worth. What did she bring back from Cairo? Calico cloth, pins, needles, women's shoes. No, she never brought anything back for other people except when neighbors specifically asked her to bring products like sugar or items like teacups. No, she never brought gunpowder, caps, or any sort of ammunition. How did she make the trip? She said she took a wagon but didn't always drive it. Sometimes she just accompanied it on horseback. She would always leave the wagon at the landing on the Missouri side and take a skiff across the river to Cairo. Did guerrillas inhabit her neighborhood? There were some about a year ago, she said, but not recently. The last time she saw any at all was about five weeks ago, when about six passed by a neighbor's house that she was visiting two miles from her home, but they didn't stop. Did she personally know any guerrillas? She knew a great many young men who left for the Southern army at the start of the war. She'd heard some of them had since become guerrillas, but she hadn't seen any of them since they left. Had anyone else ever smuggled ammunition in her wagon? "I think not," she said. "I never knew it to be done." Did she have any relatives in the Confederate army? One brother, she admitted, "but I am a Unionist. I want the South whipped." No, she didn't know of any contraband, and she didn't belong to any secret society. Jane then read the statement as her examiner had transcribed it and signed it, certifying it as true.[260]

After learning that Jane Hancock had been arrested and sent to St. Louis as a prisoner, more than thirty citizens of Cairo signed a petition asking for leniency for the young woman. The men said they believed Jane to be a loyal citizen and that the charges against her were false, having been made "through malice, hatred, and ill-will." They thought that Jane should be released and "returned to her friends." The petition reached St. Louis on September 3 and was added to her file.[261]

A bill of sale from a dry-goods store in Cairo was also added to Jane's file at some point. It was presumably meant to show that her purchases in Cairo were aboveboard, since the items listed included things like buttons, needles, and spools of thread—the very kind of items she said she usually bought—while no ammunition or similar items were on the list.[262]

On September 28, after reviewing Jane's case, Colonel Darr, acting provost marshal general, forwarded her file to Judge Advocate Lucien Eaton for trial. Two days later, Major Eaton returned the file to Darr, recommending that Jane be released immediately. Eaton noted that the charge against her

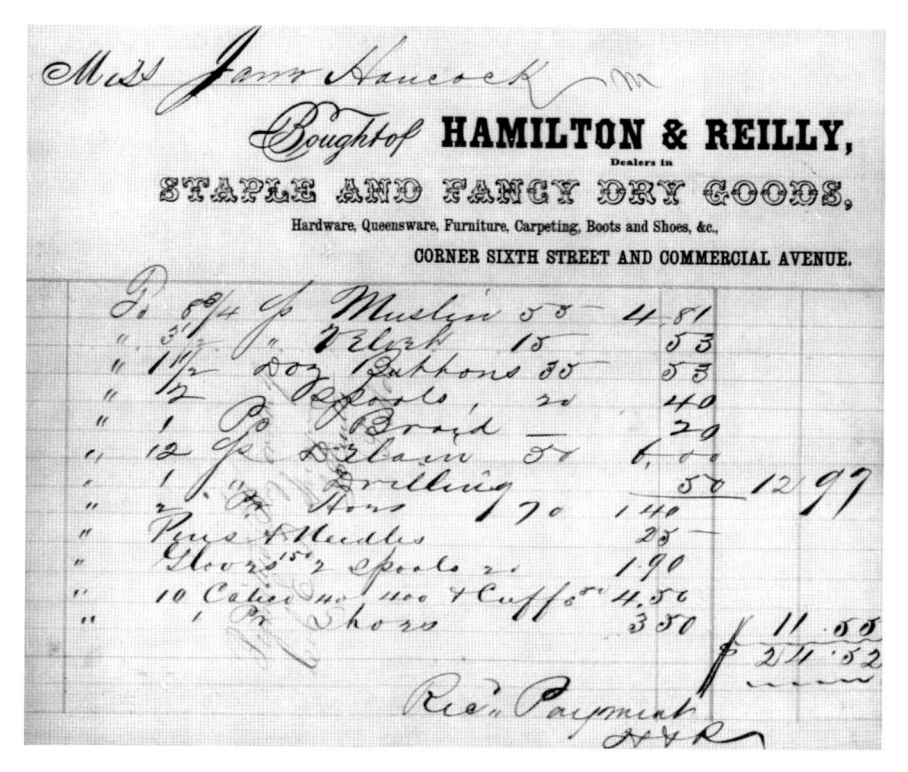

A bill of sale showing items purchased by Jane Hancock from a merchant at Cairo, Illinois. *Fold3.com.*

was an old one that was "hardly sustainable" in view of the apparent "good character of the accused." Darr immediately forwarded the file to General Rosecrans, seconding Eaton's motion. Rosecrans agreed and ordered Jane's release on her taking the oath. Signed by Darr, the order was issued on October 1, and Jane left Gratiot the same day or the next.[263]

Jane presumably returned home after her release, but what happened to her after that has not been traced. Some of her relatives, however, still lived in Mississippi County years later.[264]

15

The Mysterious Kate Beattie

A Beautifully Formed and Highly Intelligent Woman

One of the more intriguing women arrested by Union authorities in Missouri during the Civil War was Kate Beattie, not only because of the interesting circumstances of her case but also because her very identity remains something of a mystery. What is known with some certainty is that she first appeared on the scene in St. Louis in the spring of 1864. By early May, she and another woman were operating a millinery store near Fifth and Pine Streets in downtown St. Louis. Evidence suggests that she may have used the store as a front for smuggling cloth and other items to the South, but it was not until the fall of that year that she did something so audacious that Union authorities could not fail to notice her disloyal activities.[265]

On Christmas Day 1863, Major James Wilson and a detachment of Union soldiers overrode the camp of Confederate colonel Tim Reeves in southern Missouri, killing at least thirty, including, according to some sources, a number of civilians. In retaliation, Reeves ordered the executions of Wilson and six of his men after they fell into Confederate hands in the early fall of 1864. Then, in late October, as the cycle of vengeance continued, six Confederate soldiers were taken out of prison in St. Louis and executed.[266]

Enoch Wolf, a Confederate major, was also scheduled to be shot on November 11 in reprisal for Wilson's murder, and that's when Kate Beattie entered the picture. On November 10, President Lincoln wired General Rosecrans, directing that the execution be suspended until further notice. But the same day, before an order countermanding the execution had been issued, Kate sent a note to Rosecrans requesting an interview. It was signed "Mrs. Major Wolf." Rosecrans sent word that he would see the woman in the parlor of the Lindell Hotel, where both he and Kate were staying. Presenting herself as Major Wolf's wife, she begged the general to spare her husband. Rosecrans was about to tell her of the order he had received from the president, but something in her manner aroused his suspicion. He sent her to her room with the assurance that he would consider her request. She soon returned sobbing and wailing and had to be sent away again.[267]

Colonel Joseph Darr Jr., acting provost marshal general, was informed of the woman's supplications, and he visited her at the Lindell. Darr promised "Mrs. Wolf" that she could see her husband the next morning, but he shared Rosecrans's suspicion. One reason for his skepticism was that Darr knew Wolf and his wife had five children, and this woman seemed too young for that. Darr told her not to leave her room until morning, and he left a guard to watch the room. On the morning of November 11, U.S. Police chief Peter Tallon escorted the young woman to Wolf's cell. When Kate saw the major, she immediately threw her arms around him, but he reacted with a startled glance. "What," she exclaimed, "don't you know your own dear…wifey?"[268]

When Wolf asked gruffly who the hell she was, she responded with a demonstrative outburst and "cowered down under the weight of her emotions." While carrying on in such a manner, she blinked her eyes at the major and made several other "mysterious signs." Wolf finally realized that he was supposed to play along as Kate's husband, but it was too late. Tallon had also noticed her attempts to communicate clandestinely with the prisoner. The major then fell into a "fit" as Kate was led away to the provost marshal general's office.[269]

Before her arrest, Kate was wearing "a wig with luxurious black curls, which she shook over her neck and shoulders with a grace perfectly bewitching to noodle-heads." When the wig and other "mysterious swathings" with which she'd disguised herself were removed, "she grew frantic as a tigress and sprang upon Colonel Darr with the agility and ferocity of that symmetrical but treacherous animal." She pulled out a "gleaming blade" and cackled with "the very ecstasy of rage." Someone grabbed her from behind, and she was quickly placed in handcuffs. Finally her fury "dissolved in a shower of tears," and she became perfectly passive.[270]

Described as "a highly intelligent woman, not twenty years old, with light blue eyes, and light hair, cropped close to her head," the woman said her real name was Kate Beattie. Her maiden name was Brown, and she was the daughter of a Mrs. Colonel Sharp, who was then in Europe working on behalf of the Confederacy. She said she'd been educated in a Massachusetts seminary but converted to the Catholic faith. Kate wore "a rich ebony cross, which she [pressed] to her lips with fervor," and she swore that she would rather die than "reveal her purposes here" or betray her accomplices.[271]

Found on her person or in her room, however, was a treasury permit for her to buy $6,000 worth of goods to send south, and it was learned that she had purchased large quantities of military goods, as well as lace, buttons, and similar items. Although she obviously had money when making these purchases, hardly any was found among her effects after her arrest. About the only articles found were disguises of various kinds. Officials also learned that her "rebel headquarters" was located at the millinery on Fifth Street.[272]

After her arrest, Kate was taken to Gratiot Street Prison and held there in irons, but she remained defiant, telling "the military authorities, hell and the devil to do…their damndest." When Griffin Frost, held prisoner at the nearby Alton Military Prison, learned of Mrs. Beattie's fate, he vented his anger at what he saw as the cruelty of the Union justice system. "We are in the full blaze of the nineteenth century," he wrote derisively in his journal. "Women wearing balls and chains, as political offenders."[273]

When Kate first represented herself as Major Wolf's wife, she claimed she'd been living at Pilot Knob with a family named Foster and that General Price had sent her word from Marais des Cygnes, Kansas, that if Major Wolf were spared, the killer of Major Wilson would be turned over to Union authorities. Investigation revealed that no such family lived at Pilot Knob and that Price was nowhere near Marais des Cygnes at the time he supposedly sent his message.[274]

So, who exactly was Kate Beattie? A St. Louis correspondent, writing to a Cincinnati newspaper a few days after her arrest, offered further clues as to her character and her origins, suggesting that she was the wife of Buck Beattie (aka Tuck Beattie), a notorious guerrilla leader "famous in the South-West." She had supposedly written a book on slavery called *Woman's Fate* and was well known to and "highly esteemed by all the rebel Generals in the South-West." She was "beautifully formed" with "a dash and abandon of manner well calculated to carry her through." The correspondent added:

> Mrs. Beattie is one of the most…shrewd, successful and daring female rebel agents discovered since the breaking out of the war. She came up the river about a year ago with a long haired Southern doctor, who pretended to have just met her on the boat, and to have been smitten with her charms.

She then told that she had married rather romantically a Captain in the Southern army, but had separated from him and was on her way to Paris, to acquire the French language, and all the other polite accomplishments of the gentler sex.[275]

A few days after the correspondent wrote his letter, a St. Louis newspaper reprinted an ad that had appeared in a Memphis newspaper some time earlier confirming part of what the correspondent said and giving additional clues as to Kate's identity. Placed by a man representing himself as a Federal detective, the ad sought information concerning the whereabouts of "Mrs. Kate Beattie, wife of Capt. Tuck Beattie, of Lexington, Mo.…Mrs. Beattie is about five feet four inches tall, has light blue eyes, hair closely shingled, and a scar upon the right cheek. She is rather eccentric, intelligent, and prepossessing in manners."[276]

Kate's penchant for duplicity and the difficulty in confirming the sketchy details about her that she and others provided at the time of her arrest make it hard to say what her true origins were. Enoch Wolf, the man she tried to save, offered the strongest clues in the story of his ordeal that he told after the war. He said that Kate's maiden name was McCutcheon and that she grew up in Independence County, Arkansas. He was acquainted with her stepfather, whose name was indeed Sharp, and he also confirmed that she had married a man named Buck Batie. Except for the part about Kate having grown up in Independence County, Wolf's recollection is largely corroborated by the county's marriage records, which show a marriage on May 28, 1863, between Cate McCutcheon of Tennessee and Captain Thomas Beater (*sic*) of Missouri.[277]

The day after Kate was arrested, Maria Ackrell, whom Kate had engaged to do sewing and dressmaking for her, was arrested and charged with attempted smuggling. But in early December, she was released after taking an oath of allegiance and later the same month was acquitted of the charge.[278]

Kate's trial by military commission was scheduled to begin on January 7, 1865, but she was granted a continuance until the ninth, because she had not been allowed to see or write to her counsel until the day before her trial was scheduled to begin. The charges against her were violating the laws of war, being a spy, and engaging in "fraudulent practices." Specifically, she had attempted on or about November 1 to pass large quantities of military cloth and trimmings for military clothing through Federal lines to the "rebel enemies," had lurked about Federal fortifications and encampments in late October as a Confederate spy, and had falsely represented herself to Union officials in early November as Major Wolf's wife in an effort to help him escape or avoid the death sentence to which he had been condemned. Kate pleaded not guilty to the first two charges but guilty to the third.[279]

Seeking to bolster the charge against Kate of attempting to smuggle military clothing, the prosecution called as witnesses several merchants or businesspeople from whom Kate had purchased fabric and notions. All testified that she had made such purchases, but, on cross-examination, they generally agreed that she had not been secretive about the transactions, as they had taken place openly while other customers were nearby.[280]

When Major Wolf was called to the stand, he claimed that, as far as he knew, he had never seen Kate before. Even when instructed to look at the accused more closely, he still said he didn't recall having ever seen her. Perhaps his task was made more difficult by the fact that, when he'd seen Kate on the day she attempted to rescue him, she was wearing a wig and was otherwise disguised, whereas during her trial her hair was cut short. On cross-examination, he admitted that his mind had not been clear since his confinement.[281]

Most of the defense witnesses were Federal officers or officials who testified to the harsh treatment Kate had received since her incarceration. Among them were G.T. Dudley, a U.S. Army surgeon; Michael Walsh, keeper of the female portion of Gratiot Street Prison; and Robert Allen, overall head of the Gratiot Street Prison. All agreed that Kate was placed in handcuffs with a ball and chain around her leg when she first came to the prison and that she was kept in that condition for several weeks, although their recollections differed slightly on the exact length of time. She was kept in solitary confinement in a small room separate from the main prison, and she was given only bread and water during the first couple of days of her imprisonment, all of this despite the fact that she had never tried to escape or been unruly or disrespectful. Captain Allen explained that the instructions for her harsh treatment came with her order of commitment and were issued by Colonel Darr. Curiously, another defense witness was James Bagwill, Zaidee's father. He testified that during the several weeks that Kate stayed at his Oliver Street Hotel he had never seen her behave in a secretive manner and that she always "appeared to be very much of a lady."[282]

In her closing statement on January 10, Kate said that, since she had not been afforded an opportunity to meet with counsel until January 8, and then only in the presence of guards, she was unable to prepare an adequate defense. However, it was not up to her to prove her innocence, she said. It was up to the prosecution to prove her guilt, and the court had not met that standard, because she simply did not do the things she'd been accused of, except for her rash attempt to free Major Wolf in a moment of "frenzied sympathy" for him and his dire situation. Her purchases of fabric, trimming, and other notions had been for her own use, she said, pointing out that everything she bought was used in dressmaking as well as making military outfits. She denied the charge, leveled by one of the merchants, that she'd told him she had previously bought $6,000 worth of goods under a government permit. Kate resented the "thrilling and glowing falsehoods" that had been published about her in newspapers "in order to poison the public mind against me." She blamed the bad publicity on "the prejudice and malignity of two officers no longer in command" (no doubt a reference to General Rosecrans and Colonel Darr). She pointed out that she had done most of her shopping at some of the most patriotic stores in St. Louis, as demonstrated by their display of U.S. flags and symbols. If she were smuggling goods, why would she have patronized those establishments? she asked rhetorically. And if she were really a spy as she was accused of being, there was no way she would have exposed herself by trying to free Major Wolf. She had been subjected to cruel punishment only because the two officers to whom she'd previously alluded were angry at her for deceiving them during her attempt to free Major Wolf.[283]

At the close of the proceedings on January 10, Kate was found not guilty of the first two charges against her but guilty of the third charge, fraudulent practices, since she had already admitted impersonating Mrs. Wolf to try to free Major Wolf. The commission opted for leniency in view of the harsh treatment Kate had received prior to trial, and she was sentenced to imprisonment for one month. General Dodge remitted even that sentence and banished her immediately to the South.[284]

Apparently, some sentiment had existed among Union officials in St. Louis that Kate should receive the death penalty, because President Lincoln wired General Dodge on January 19 ordering that, if Kate were sentenced to death, Dodge should postpone any such execution until further notice. Dodge replied to the president's message on the same day he received it, informing Lincoln that Kate had already been sent south. Among other women banished at the same time as Kate were the sisters of notorious guerrilla William "Bloody Bill" Anderson.[285]

In late March 1865, Kate came back to St. Louis and either reported to the provost marshal general's office or was otherwise taken into custody. She was lodged in the Gratiot Street Prison but was released unconditionally on April 1.[286]

Left: President Abraham Lincoln interceded on Kate Beattie's behalf. *Library of Congress.*

Right: General Grenville Dodge remitted Kate's sentence to banishment after a military commission sentenced her to imprisonment. *Library of Congress.*

But Union authorities hadn't quite heard the last of Kate Beattie. On September 6, 1865, Samuel Foster complained to the provost marshal's office about a Mrs. Beatty, very likely Kate, who had taken a room at the same boardinghouse where he lived. She had requested a private room because she was writing a history of the war, but Foster thought she was up to no good, because she had been consorting with former Confederate officers and had bragged that one of them had influence at West Point.[287]

Apparently nothing came of the matter, and Kate was not heard from again until Enoch Wolf saw her several years after the war and observed that she "still bore on her wrists scars caused by sores made by the handcuffs which were fastened tightly around her wrists" during her confinement in St. Louis.[288]

Although Wolf's recollections of Kate Beattie, reinforced by Independence County marriage records, solve the problem of her origins to some extent, much about her remains a mystery. Who were Kate's parents? How old was she, where in Tennessee was she from, and what happened to her after Wolf's postwar encounter with her? These and other questions remain unanswered.

16

Amanda Cranwill

A Fair and Buxom Widow of the South

Women arrested in Civil War Missouri for deliberate acts of subversion like smuggling mail tended to receive harsher punishments than those arrested merely for feeding their brothers in the bush. But the comparative severity of their offenses wasn't the only determining factor in their differing sentences. Those who committed deliberate acts of subversion were often older and more set in their devotion to the Southern cause than those who aided guerrillas because of family ties, and they were less likely to retreat into helpless womanhood after they were arrested. They were loath to express regret for the acts that got them into trouble in the first place, and their persistent attitude of rebellion only got them into deeper trouble. Such seems to have been the case with Amanda Cranwill (aka Cranwell or Cranville), who was banished to the South at the same time as Kate Beattie.

The daughter of David and Rachel Winchester, Amanda was born about 1827 in Georgia. She married Samuel Cranwill in New Orleans in 1846. By 1850, the couple was living in St. Louis, where Samuel was a forwarding and commission merchant. In 1861, the couple separated because of "unfortunate difficulties between them." Amanda remained in St. Louis for a short while before returning to her native Georgia. She also spent time in New Orleans and Florida before teaching school for a year in Summerfield, Alabama.[289]

In August 1864, Amanda determined to come back to St. Louis, because, according to her story, she'd heard that Cranwill was dead and she wanted to check on any inheritance she might be entitled to. Amanda reached Meridian, Mississippi, in late August and obtained a pass from Confederate officials to travel to Grenada, 140 miles to the northwest. At Grenada, she received another pass. The endorsement on the pass explaining that Mrs. Cranwill was on her way to St. Louis to settle her late husband's estate suggests that, if she had an ulterior motive for making the trip, even Confederate officers who passed her through the lines might have been kept in the dark about it. Although Amanda was careful to obtain Confederate passes during her trip north, she crossed into Federal territory without a Union pass. She laid over in Memphis for about two weeks and finally arrived in St. Louis in mid- to late October.[290]

On her arrival, she wrote to a Memphis bank official to make arrangements for him to send her over $300 in Confederate money, presumably for her return trip to the South. During her five-week sojourn in St. Louis, Amanda stayed first in the Planter's Hotel and later at a boardinghouse. She rented a piano and practiced playing it, and she took voice lessons from Madame Carlotta Pozzoni, a nationally known operatic performer and St. Louis resident. She also found time to go shopping and purchased a number of articles, including a pistol.[291]

Sometime in early November, Amanda hired a St. Louis carpenter to make a secret compartment in the bottom of her trunk. After doing the work, the shopkeeper reported the suspicious job to Union authorities, and they began keeping an eye on Amanda. On November 28, Amanda went to see Judge John Crumm and learned, according to her story, that she had no settlement forthcoming from her husband's estate. About the same time as her visit to the judge, she attempted to obtain a pass to return south, but Colonel Darr was "very busy and excited" when she called at the provost marshal general's office. She also went to General Rosecrans's office but was unable to see him. Nevertheless, on November 30, she had her luggage sent to the steamboat *Graham*. When she boarded later the same day, U.S. policeman Augustus Coring was there waiting for her.[292]

Coring demanded to search Amanda's trunk. He found little to raise suspicion until he discovered the false bottom. Using a screwdriver to remove it, he found the pistol, three boxes of cartridges, eight boxes of gun caps, the Confederate money, letters, poems, and papers. Coring took Amanda into custody and reported to Union authorities that she had tried to bribe him, offering him the pistol or anything else he wanted not to turn her in. Considering the circumstances of Amanda's arrest, Union authorities obviously did not believe her story that she'd come to St. Louis only to

Planter's House Hotel, where Amanda Cranwill stayed during part of her St. Louis sojourn. *Missouri Historical Society, St. Louis.*

check on property she might be entitled to from her husband, and she was immediately lodged in the Gratiot Street Female Prison. Union officials thought Amanda might be concealing other letters besides those found in her trunk, but a search of her person turned up no additional correspondence.[293]

In describing Amanda's arrest the next day, the *Daily Missouri Democrat* called her "a fair and buxom widow of the South, possessing charms that would almost woo an anchorite from his beads and seclusion." However, the editors were pleased to report that, because her mission had been such a "deplorable failure," the cultured Mrs. Cranwill now mourned in prison "the fatality that led her to court such danger in unlawful enterprises."[294]

Amanda was examined on November 30, the day she was arrested, and again on December 19. During the first interview, she told her examiner she had lost her husband, letting him assume that she was a widow. When pressed on why she'd gone to see Judge Crumm, however, she finally admitted that her husband had sued her for divorce and she'd gone to

This sketch showing Union authorities issuing passes at St. Louis depicts a scene similar to what Amanda Cranwill may have encountered when she sought a pass to return to the South. *Library of Congress.*

the judge to see whether the divorce was final. She'd heard her estranged husband was dead, but she didn't know for sure. Amanda said she could not take an oath of allegiance to the United States, because to do so would mean "forswearing the country of my birth." During the second examination, Amanda explained that she'd bought the gun so that she would have it for personal protection when she got to the South. She'd told Officer Coring a slight variation of the same story—that she'd bought it for her mother. The only letters she'd brought with her from the South were one from Mrs. Bibb in Alabama to Mrs. Bibb's mother in New York and one from Mrs. Telfair, also of Alabama, to a different woman in New York. Amanda had mailed the letters once she reached St. Louis, and the New York parties had sent answering letters to her. Those were the only letters she was taking back when she was arrested. Why did Amanda stay so long in St. Louis? her examiner asked. Because she wanted to take music lessons from Madame Pozzoni. Why did she wait until just a couple of days before departing to contact Judge Crumm? Because she didn't want her old acquaintances to know she was in town. About the only people she saw during her stay were her landlord, her music teacher, and the piano tuner.[295]

During the second interrogation, Amanda complained to her examiner that one of the turnkeys at the female prison was in the habit of using "filthy, abusive and profane language" to her and some of the other lady prisoners, and that he otherwise mistreated them. The complaint was referred to R.C. Allen, captain in charge of Gratiot Street Prison. He reported that Mrs. Cranwill "made herself conspicuous by her persistent contrariness" and that she herself was guilty of using abusive language toward the guards. Allen thought she "delighted in giving us all the trouble in her power." After Allen's report, the investigation into Amanda's complaint was promptly dropped.[296]

On December 19, the same day as Amanda's examination, her estranged husband, Samuel Cranwill, who was very much alive, wrote a letter from Montreal, Canada, to Judge Crumm. He'd seen a report of Amanda's arrest in a St. Louis newspaper, and he thought she might not be guilty of the charges against her. He had, indeed, taken out a life-insurance policy some years earlier in his wife's favor, and he was aware, too, that a rumor had recently circulated in the South that he was dead. Despite the "troubles and disgrace" Amanda had brought on him, Cranwill did not want to see her suffer for something she might not be guilty of. He asked that Judge Crumm see what he could do for the "unfortunate woman" but not to tell her that her estranged husband had anything to do with the matter.[297]

Crumm, in turn, wrote to the provost marshal general's office requesting an interview with Mrs. Cranwill. He said that both she and her husband had been "very much esteemed" when they lived together in St. Louis before their marital difficulties. He would like to check into her case, but he might decide he didn't want to represent her after interviewing her.[298]

Amanda's trial for smuggling and violating the laws of war took place on December 23. One of the main witnesses against her was Augustus Coring, the policeman who'd searched her belongings aboard the steamboat. Amanda especially took issue with Coring's testimony that she'd offered to give him her trunk or anything in it to avoid arrest. The defense argued, both during cross-examination of the witness and in Amanda's closing statement, that she had not resisted arrest but had only pleaded with Coring not to subject her to any "unnecessary exposure" aboard the steamboat. She had suggested that he take her trunk or any of its contents to the provost marshal's office and she would follow voluntarily, but he had construed this as a bribe. Amanda also emphasized in her closing statement that she had intended to get a pass to go south and had tried repeatedly to do so before deciding to leave without one, as she was running low on U.S. currency. The commission was little swayed, as it found her guilty of the smuggling charge, although it did acquit on the charge of violating the laws of war. She was sentenced to imprisonment for the duration of the war.[299]

Amanda probably didn't help her cause by her actions just a few days before the sentence was to be promulgated. On the morning of January 14, 1865, Captain Allen had a U.S. flag suspended from his office window and another suspended from the window of Amanda's cell at the female prison across the street. Just a few minutes after the flag was put up in her window, Amanda threw it into the street below. Allen had her placed in handcuffs for the insult she had "offered to the flag of our country," and he reported the matter to the provost marshal general.[300]

Despite Amanda's defiant behavior, when the proceedings of her trial were promulgated on January 18, 1865, General Dodge disapproved the sentence and, instead, banished her to Dixie. Amanda left the next day on the same steamboat that took Kate Beattie down the river.[301]

Once the war ended, Amanda Cranwill promptly resumed her artistic pursuits. Under the heading "A Fine Concert, " the *Memphis Bulletin* reported on May 27, 1865: "The musical public are somewhat excited over a concert proposed to be given in the Greenlaw Opera House on next Tuesday evening under the auspices of Mrs. Cranwell [*sic*], who intends to devote herself to teaching music in our city."[302]

Amanda, "a soprano of fine voice and great talent," continued to perform in concert and to teach vocal, guitar, and piano music at various academies throughout the South over the next twenty or thirty years. She also found time for romance, remarrying once to a man named Wilson and another time to a man named Richardson. Amanda died sometime after 1906.[303]

17

Mary Jane Duncan

Sam Hildebrand's "Sister"

Even in the late winter and early spring of 1865, as it became increasingly obvious that a Union victory in the Civil War was just a matter of time, Missouri women with Southern sympathies continued to come into the clutches of Union justice. Mary Jane Duncan of Madison County was just one example. Although Mary had been outspoken in her support of the Confederacy for a long time, no one turned her in for her disloyalty until some of her neighbors were robbed by guerrillas two months before the war ended, and the neighbors suspected that Mary might have somehow abetted the bushwhackers.[304]

Born in Tennessee about 1834, Mary Campbell came to Missouri with her family after 1850. She married Jonathan Marion Duncan in Madison County in February 1855, and they took up residence on a farm about four miles west of Fredericktown, the county seat.[305]

In mid-February 1865, a band of guerrillas carried out a raid in Madison County, robbing Mary's neighbors Andrew Bray and James Duncan. (It's not clear whether James Duncan was related to Mary's husband.) The bushwhackers held up Bray and his family at gunpoint and threatened to blow their brains out. Duncan was away from the house when they came to his place, but they robbed his wife, Elizabeth, and told her they'd kill her husband if they could find him.[306]

Based on statements Mary previously made in support of guerrillas, she quickly came under suspicion of having somehow aided or encouraged the guerrillas in the raid. On March 1, several of her neighbors gave statements to W.C. Shattuck, assistant provost marshal at Fredericktown, swearing to Mary's disloyalty. Harriet Wallace said she'd heard Mary "express herself as a Rebel very often." Nancy Atterbury said she'd heard Mary say in the summer of 1864 that she was Sam Hildebrand's "sister," which Nancy took to mean "friend." Hildebrand was a notorious guerrilla leader in southeast Missouri, but it's not certain whether his band carried out the mid-February 1865 raid in the Duncan neighborhood. Nancy added that Mary said that if she had a brother, she would encourage him to join Hildebrand and that she would do so herself if she were a man. Nancy also heard Mary threaten to have Hildebrand's guerrillas pay Elizabeth Duncan a visit. Margaret Furguson said she overheard Elizabeth Duncan confront Mary about whether she'd made such a threat and that Mary did not deny it, exclaiming that if she wanted to bring the guerrillas on Elizabeth, she would "be God damned" if she wouldn't do it. Elizabeth herself said she heard Mary Duncan say that she was a Rebel and always would be, that she would give information to guerrillas about every "Black Republican" she knew, and that she dared Elizabeth to report her for it.[307]

Mary Jane Duncan considered herself a "sister" of guerrilla chief Sam Hildebrand. *Courtesy of the Daily Journal Online.*

On March 1, the same day he took the statements, Lieutenant Shattuck forwarded them up the chain of command, and they reached St. Louis on or about March 7. On March 9, General Dodge ordered that Mary Duncan be brought to St. Louis and then banished to the South. Arrested on the seventeenth, she was taken to Pilot Knob, where she spent the night. The next day, she was escorted to St. Louis and committed to the Gratiot Street Female Prison. The unidentified officer who forwarded her from Pilot Knob sent a letter with her escort asking whether General Dodge might modify his order of banishment to allow her to be sent to Illinois instead of to the South and requesting that her husband and three small children, who otherwise would suffer from her absence, be allowed to join her.[308]

The officer who sent Mary to St. Louis was hardly alone in his petition for special consideration in her case. Mary herself wrote to James H.

Baker, the provost marshal general, almost immediately on her arrival at the female prison, asking for a speedy trial so that she might return to her children. She also told Colonel Baker she was in need of clothes. She signed the letter "Jane Duncan."[309]

On March 21, just three days later, at least five of Mary's neighbors swore out affidavits before a Madison County justice of the peace vindicating her loyalty. All five said they'd never seen guerrillas at Mary's house and never heard her make any threats toward Union citizens. Most notable among the five affiants was Harriet Wallace, one of the women whose statements three weeks earlier had resulted in Mary's arrest in the first place. Mrs. Wallace now said, "I think her arrest was occasioned more from old grudges than from feeding guerrillas." One of the other four affiants was Harriet's husband, William Wallace. One wonders whether she had a real change of heart or was just doing what Mr. Wallace wanted.[310]

The five affidavits attesting to Mary's loyalty were forwarded to St. Louis on March 25, along with statements by at least two acknowledged Union men vouching for the loyalty of the affiants. Then, on April 6, a petition, signed by at least thirty Madison County citizens and asking that Mary's family be allowed to accompany her if she was to be banished, was sent to St. Louis.[311]

Mary's file was temporarily misplaced after it reached St. Louis, resulting in inaction in her case for a couple of weeks. After the file turned up, Mary was interviewed on April 22. She said she had "never used any disloyal language that [she] knew of," was not a Southern sympathizer, and wanted to see the Confederacy put down. She said she didn't even know who had reported her.[312]

In late April, Mary's husband sent a telegram to the Gratiot Street Female Prison informing Mary that he would be at Chester, Illinois, on May 2 with their kids and for her to meet them there if the requested modification of her banishment order was granted. Mary replied on April 28 that she would be there, assuming she was released in time.[313]

But forces were already afoot that would make the trip to Illinois unnecessary. With peace treaties having already been signed, Union officials tended to be more lenient than they might have been just months before. It no doubt also helped that so many of Mary's friends and neighbors had come to her aid during her time of distress. On April 29, Assistant Provost Marshal C.W. Davis wrote to Colonel Baker recommending that the banishment order be modified in consideration of Mary's "helpless and destitute" children. Instead, on May 1, General Dodge revoked the banishment order altogether, releasing Mary to go home, and she walked out of Gratiot Street Prison a free woman the next day.[314]

Mary returned to Madison County and resumed residence there. Her husband died sometime before 1880, when she was still living in Madison County as a widow. What happened to Mary after 1880 has not been traced.[315]

Epilogue

> *Bravely they bared their arms to the fight,*
> *Soldiers in gray, for woman and right.*
> *Alas! not always can right be might;*
> *Over the South is night.*

In 1895, Amanda Cranwill, drawing partly on the half-remembered poems she had lost at the time of her arrest in St. Louis, published a book of poetry, *Scattered Leaves: Poems from a Collection of Poems Lost during the War*. Although considered a rare book, the collection is still housed in at least twenty-five libraries.

The stanza above is taken from one of the poems, "Who Was She?" It was dedicated to a woman who tended sick and wounded Confederate soldiers during the Civil War and who was subsequently buried, at her request, among Southern soldiers in a Louisville cemetery.[316]

Amanda, of course, took on a more daring role to aid the Confederacy than tending wounded soldiers. In an introductory note to one of the other poems in the volume, she admitted that she had been on a "mission" for the South when she trekked to St. Louis in 1864. "The Yankees caught me and caged me," she remembered. This, however, was the only allusion in the book to Amanda's clash with Union authorities or to her wartime imprisonment. Elsewhere in the little volume, notably the preface, she emphasized her love for the South, but she recalled her wartime experience within the same context that she saw the unknown nurse's role—as that of a helpmate for the "soldiers in gray" who were fighting "for woman and right." Although Amanda had complained at the time she was imprisoned of the mistreatment and abusive language directed toward her by one of the guards at the Gratiot Street Female Prison, thirty years later she said nothing of the hardship or ordeal involved in her Civil War incarceration. In fact, she barely mentioned it at all, making only the one indirect allusion to it.[317]

Thus it was with most of the other Southern women who clashed with Union authority in Missouri during the Civil War. Many had played daring roles in active support of the Confederacy, such as spying, carrying mail, and smuggling goods. Further asserting their autonomy, some, like Maggie Creath and Emily Weaver, rode horses, carried guns, or engaged in other activities normally thought unladylike. For the Rebel women of Missouri, their resistance to Union authority often turned into a harrowing experience, but it was also an empowering one.

Cover of *Scattered Leaves*, Amanda Cranwill's anthology of poems, published in 1895. Public domain.

However, their newfound agency was more thrust upon them than sought. It was demanded by circumstance, not by them. Most of the lady Rebels of Missouri were far from women's rights advocates. For instance, Mary Cleveland's patron Willis Reynolds told Provost Marshal General James Broadhead that Mary, on religious grounds, could not take an oath of allegiance to the Union, but there was more to her refusal than that. In her letter to Reynolds, before he intervened on her behalf with Broadhead, Mary made it clear that she also would not take an oath of allegiance to the Confederacy. "It is too much like woman's rights," she said. Of course, the Union's mere expectation that Mary should take an oath was an implicit recognition of her personhood, but her reasons for refusing such an oath make it clear that, even though Mary was very active in her support of the Confederacy, political autonomy was not something she sought.[318]

Once the war was over, the Southern women who had clashed with Union authority usually returned to traditional, domestic roles, and they contributed to the myth of the Lost Cause in how they recollected their wartime experiences. Although the South may have been defeated by the superior might of the Union, as the Amanda Cranwill poem suggests, the

Confederate cause remained right. Southern women in general and those who had clashed with Union authority in particular played an important role in perpetuating this view in the postwar years. The women who had been arrested while carrying out daring missions for the Confederacy certainly did not want their devotion to the South forgotten, but they tended not to emphasize the active roles they had taken. Like Amanda Cranwill, some scarcely recalled their ordeals at all. Others, like Lucie Nicholson, offered more details about their Civil War exploits, but even Lucie saw herself largely as a victim. For the women to emphasize their own contributions and their own tribulations would have been to minimize the sacrifices of Confederate soldiers. So they framed their postwar stories within the context of redeeming their men, whom they remembered as noble warriors fighting for their families.[319]

Indeed, "Confederate cause" came to be viewed by many Southerners, especially in areas like Missouri where irregular warfare flourished, almost synonymously with "defense of home." The Civil War, as Amanda Cranwill remembered, involved "soldiers in gray" fighting for "woman and right."[320]

This understanding of the war was probably even more prevalent in the countryside of out-state Missouri than it was in St. Louis. For women who had clashed with Union authorities during the Civil War primarily for feeding and harboring bushwhackers, the retreat into apolitical womanhood and the ready adoption of the myth of the Lost Cause was a relatively easy transition, because many had never stepped out of their traditional roles to begin with. The guerrilla war in Missouri was a household war, and many of the women who were arrested only for feeding and harboring bushwhackers were merely fulfilling their normal, domestic duty of caring for their friends and loved ones. However, even those who had been more purposeful agents of the Confederate war effort and had been arrested for offenses like spying or carrying mail in and around St. Louis readily surrendered whatever political power the circumstances of war had afforded them, and they, too, embraced the myth of the noble warrior fighting to protect their homes and families.[321]

Notes

Short forms, such as an author's last name only, are often used to cite sources. For frequently cited sources, the following abbreviations or shortened forms are used.

Confederate Records	Civil War Service Records—Confederate
CMCF	Court Martial Case Files
Ind. Cit.	Provost Marshals' File of Papers Relating to Individual Citizens
MSPD	Missouri State Prison Database
OR	*The War of the Rebellion: A Compilation of the Official Records of the Union and Confederate Armies*
Powell Diary	Lizzie M. Powell Hereford Prison Diary
Two or More	Union Provost Marshal Papers, Two or More Civilians
SLDMD	*St. Louis Daily Missouri Democrat*
SLDMR	*St. Louis Daily Missouri Republican*
Subversion	Civil War Subversion Investigations
Unfiled	Unfiled Papers and Slips Belonging in Confederate Compiled Service Records

Introduction

1. "Atlas of U.S. Presidential Elections."
2. I consulted a number of sources in writing this summary of the early days of the Civil War in Missouri, including Snead's *Fight for Missouri*, Violette's *History of Missouri* and Sutherland's *Savage Conflict*.

1. Jane Haller

3. Edwards, *Noted Guerrillas*, 52, 54; U.S. Census 1860.
4. U.S. Census, 1850, 1860; Find A Grave, Memorial #13476556.
5. U.S. Census, 1860; Find A Grave, #13476556.
6. Ind. Cit., Wash Haller.
7. Ibid.
8. Ind. Cit., Bill Haller; *Official Army Register of Volunteer Forces*, 30.
9. Ind. Cit., Bill Haller.
10. Ind. Cit., Sarah Cox; Subversion, Jane Haller.
11. Subversion, Jane Haller.
12. Subversion, Jane Haller; Burch, *Charles W. Quantrell*, 127–28, 159; Find A Grave, #100666844.

2. Lizzie Powell

13. Ind. Cit., Lizzie Powell.
14. U.S. Census, 1850; Two or More, F1591, Frames 847–48.
15. Ind. Cit, Mog Creath; Powell Diary, 2.
16. Powell Diary, 3.
17. Ibid., 3–7.
18. Powell Diary, 8–10; Two or More, F1589, Frame 1204.
19. Powell Diary, 11–12.
20. Two or More, F1589, Frames 1205–7.
21. Powell Diary, 14–16.
22. Ibid., 17–18.
23. Ibid., 18–20.
24. Two or More, F1589, Frames 1202–3.
25. Powell Diary, 24–25.
26. Ibid., 26.

27. *OR*, Series 2, 5:78.
28. Two or More, F1589, Frames 1199–200.
29. Powell Diary, 27–28; Ind. Cit., Lizzie Powell.
30. Ind. Cit., Lizzie Powell.
31. Ind. Cit., Lizzie Powell; Ind. Cit., Lizzie M. Powell; Powell Diary, 29–31.
32. Powell Diary, 38–43; Ind. Cit., Lizzie Powell.
33. Ind. Cit., Lizzie M. Powell; Powell Diary, 45.
34. Powell Diary, 51; "Biographical Sketch," Hereford, Papers; U.S. Census, 1870; *Kansas City Times*, September 7, 1877; *St. Joseph Gazette*, November 14, 1877.

3. Augusta and Zaidee Bagwill

35. Ind. Cit., James H. Bagwell; Ind. Cit, Jas. H. Bagwell.
36. Missouri Marriages; U.S. Census, 1850; CMCF, LL 548; Two or More, F1099, Frame 1203; Ind. Cit., Augusta W. Bagwill.
37. CMCF, LL 548.
38. Ind. Cit., Augusta W. Bagwill.
39. Ibid.
40. Ind. Cit., Zaidee J. Bagwill.
41. Ibid.
42. Ibid.; Nichols, *Guerrilla Warfare in Civil War Missouri*, 84.
43. Ind. Cit., Augusta W. Bagwill; Ind. Cit., Zaidee J. Bagwill; CMCF, LL 548.
44. *OR*, Series 1, Vol. 34, Pt. 2, 102–3; Ind. Cit., Zaidee J. Bagwill; CMCF, LL 548.
45. Ind. Cit, Augusta W. Bagwell; Ind. Cit., Augusta W. Bagwill; Ind. Cit., Zaidee J. Bagwell; Ind. Cit., Zaidee J. Bagwill; SLDMR, June 7, 19, 1863; CMCF, LL 548.
46. Ind. Cit., Augusta M. Bagwill; SLMDR, October 11, 1863; Confederate Records, William F. Luckett; Missouri Marriage Records; U.S. Census, 1870; Find A Grave, Memorials 105860945, 16300757.

4. Addie Haynes

47. Unfiled, Addie M. Haynes; Unfiled, Addie M. Haines, 251934428.
48. Unfiled, Ada M. Haines; U.S. Census, 1860; *SLDMD*, July 16, 1858.

49. Haynes Papers, P.S. Sandridge letters, March 6, 1862, March 21, 1862 and C.B. Alexander letter, June 1, 1862; Unfiled, Addie M. Haines.
50. Unfiled, Addie M. Haines.
51. Ibid.
52. Unfiled, Addie M. Haynes.
53. "Gratiot Street Prisoner List."
54. *SLDMR*, May 14, 1863; "General Orders No. 100."
55. Unfiled, Ada M. Haines. The transcription of Addie's statement identifies the town where she spent most of her banishment as Columbus, Kentucky, but it's clear from the context and other evidence that it must have been Columbus, Mississippi.
56. Ibid.
57. Ibid.
58. Ibid.
59. Unfiled, Ada M. Haines; Unfiled, Ada Haynes.
60. Unfiled, Ada M. Haines; *SLDMD*, July 22, 1864.
61. *SLDMD*, July 22, 1864; Haynes Papers, "Typescript History"; Unfiled, Ada M. Haines.
62. Ind. Cit., Ada M. Haynes.
63. U.S. Census, 1880, 1900, 1910, 1920; Haynes Papers, "Typescript History"; Find A Grave, Memorial #155593863.

5. Lucie Nicholson

64. U.S. Census, 1850; Slave Schedule, 1850, 1860; *Lathrop (MO) Optimist*, April 5, 1923; *Kansas City (MO) Times*, April 6, 1923; *St. Louis Post-Dispatch*, April 4, 1923; *History of Clinton County*, Biographical, 38–39.
65. *History of Clinton County*, Biographical, 39; Nancy Chapman Jones Letters.
66. Ind. Cit., Lucie Nicholson; *History of Clinton County*, Biographical, 39; *Women of Missouri in the Civil War*, "Reminiscences of Mrs. Lucy Nickolson Lindsay" [hereafter "Reminiscences of Mrs. Lucy Nickolson Lindsay"].
67. Ind. Cit., Lucie Nicholson.
68. Ibid.
69. Ibid.
70. Ind. Cit., Lucie Nicholson; "Gratiot Street Prisoner List"; Unfiled, Mary Louden; Nichols, *Guerrilla Warfare in Civil War Missouri*, 84; "Reminiscences of Mrs. Lucy Nickolson Lindsay."
71. *SLDMD*, May 14, 1863; Ind. Cit., Lucie Nicholson.

72. Ind. Cit., Lucie Nicholson.
73. *SLDMR*, May 10, 14, 1863.
74. "Reminiscences of Mrs. Lucy Nickolson"; *SLDMD*, May 14, 1863.
75. "Reminiscences of Mrs. Lucy Nickolson Lindsay"; Unfiled, John Q. Burbridge; *History of Clinton County*, Biographical, 40.
76. *History of Clinton County*, Biographical, 40; "Reminiscences of Mrs. Lucy Nickolson Lindsay"; Ellis, "1863 Civil War Diary."
77. *History of Clinton County*, Biographical, 40; Find A Grave, Memorial 17628989; U.S. Census, 1910, *Kansas City Star*, April 9, 1915.
78. *St. Louis Post-Dispatch*, April 4, 1923.
79. *Lathrop (MO) Optimist*, April 5, 1923.

6. Hattie Snodgrass

80. Ind. Cit., Harriet Snodgrass; U.S. Census, 1850, 1860.
81. Ind. Cit., Harriet Snodgrass; U.S. Census, 1850, 1860; *First Annual Report of the General Superintendent*, 107.
82. Ind. Cit., Harriet Snodgrass.
83. Ibid.; Moore, "Corrections of Two Articles," 40.
84. Ind. Cit., Harriet Snodgrass.
85. Ibid.
86. Ibid.
87. Ibid.
88. Ibid.
89. Ibid.
90. Ibid.
91. Ibid.; Moore, "Corrections of Two Articles," 40.
92. Ind. Cit., Harriet Snodgrass; Unfiled, J.Q. Burbridge.
93. Unfiled, J.Q. Burbridge.
94. *SLDMD*, May 14, 1863.
95. Unfiled, J.Q. Burbridge.
96. Ibid.
97. Unfiled, Burbridge; Pinnell, *Serving with Honor*.
98. *Women of Missouri in the Civil War*, Mrs. C.C. (Hannah) Rainwater, "Reminiscences from 1861 to 1865."
99. Ibid.
100. Ibid.
101. Ibid.

102. Ibid.
103. Ibid.
104. U.S. Census, 1880; Thomas, *History of St. Louis County*, 102.

7. Marion W. Vail

105. U.S. Census, 1860; *1852 St. Louis City Directory*; *1854 St. Louis City Directory*.
106. U.S. Census, 1860; Ind. Cit., Marion W. Vail; Ind. Cit., M.W. Vail; Grimes, 49, 96–97. Commissioned as an officer in the Confederate army and designated as the "official mail carrier" for General Sterling Price's army, Grimes sometimes referred to Marion as "Aunt," but it's not clear they were actually related.
107. Ind. Cit., Marion W. Vail.
108. Ibid.
109. Ibid.
110. Ibid.
111. Ibid.; Ind. Cit., Marionne W. Vail.
112. Ind. Cit., Cora O. Vail.
113. Ibid.
114. Ind. Cit., M.W. Vail; Ind. Cit., Marion W. Vail.
115. Ind. Cit., M.W. Vail.
116. Ibid.
117. Ind. Cit., Marionne W. Vail.
118. Ibid.
119. Grimes, *Absalom Grimes*, 96–99.
120. Two or More, F1598, #5084; Grimes, *Absalom Grimes*, 137–38, 144.
121. Ind. Cit., Marion W. Vail; Grimes, *Absalom Grimes*, 138.
122. Ind. Cit., Cora O. Vail.
123. Ind. Cit., M.W. Vail; Grimes, *Absalom Grimes*, 180–87.
124. Ind. Cit., M.W. Vail.
125. Ibid.
126. Ind. Cit., Vail.
127. Ind. Cit., C.O. Vail.
128. Ibid.; Ind. Cit., M.W. Vail; Grimes, *Absalom Grimes*, 205–6.
129. Ind. Cit., M.W. Vail.
130. Ind. Cit., M.W. Vail; U.S. Census, 1870, 1880, 1900.
131. Grimes, *Absalom Grimes*, 138.

8. Mary Susan F. Cleveland

132. U.S. Census, 1850, 1860; Confederate Records, Benjamin A.F. Cleveland.
133. Ind. Cit., Cleveland; Ind. Cit., Mary S.F. Cleveland.
134. Unfiled, Jane E. Cleveland; Ind. Cit., John D. Cleveland.
135. Ind. Cit., Mary Cleveland; Ind. Cit., Mary S.F. Cleveland; Ind. Cit., S.F. Cleveland.
136. Ind. Cit., S.F. Cleveland; Ind. Cit., Mary S.F. Cleveland.
137. Ind. Cit., Mary S.F. Cleveland; Ind. Cit., S.F. Cleveland.
138. Ind. Cit., Mary S.F. Cleveland; Ind. Cit., S.F. Cleveland.
139. Ind. Cit., Mary S.F. Cleveland; Ind. Cit., S.F. Cleveland.
140. Ind. Cit., S.F. Cleveland; Ind. Cit., Mary S.F. Cleveland.
141. Ind. Cit., Mary S.F. Cleveland; *Leavenworth (KS) Daily Conservative*, May 14, 1863.
142. Ind. Cit., Jane E. Cleveland.
143. Ind. Cit., Mary Cleveland; Ind. Cit, Cleveland; *SLDMR*, June 2, 1863.
144. Ind. Cit., Mary S.F. Cleveland.
145. Ind. Cit., Mary Cleveland; Ind. Cit., Mary S.F. Cleveland.
146. Ind. Cit., Mary S.F. Cleveland.
147. *St. Louis Globe-Democrat*, September 23, 1875, July 19, 1898; *St. Louis Board of Education Annual Report*, Vols. 20–21; Find A Grave, Memorial #182043961.

9. The Blennerhassett Sisters

148. *SLDMR*, November 25, 1863.
149. U.S. Census, 1850, 1860; *St. Louis Post-Dispatch*, November 2, 1890; Missouri Marriages; Find A Grave, Memorial 7247188.
150. Haynes Papers, "Transcript History"; Confederate Records, Hampton L. Boon and Edward Blennerhasset; *SLDMR*, November 24, 1863; Ind. Cit., Therese Balnnerhassett.
151. Confederate Records, Hampton L. Boon; CMCF, NN3355.
152. *SLDMR*, November 24, 1863.
153. Ind. Cit., Therse Balnnerhassett.
154. *SLDMR*, November 24 1863.
155. CMCF, NN 3355.
156. Ind. Cit., Annie B. Martin.

157. Ibid.
158. Ibid.
159. Ind. Cit., Annie B. Martin; Ind. Cit., Anna B. Martin.
160. Unfiled, Annie B. Martin. CMCF, NN 3355.
161. Lincoln, *Collected Works*.
162. Frost, *Camp and Prison Journal*, 200–6.
163. Ibid., 218–27.
164. Unfiled, Annie B. Martin; Frost, 229.
165. Frost, *Camp and Prison Journal*, 229, 238.
166. U.S. Census, 1870, 1880; *SLDMR*, October 9, 1866; *St. Louis Globe-Democrat*, September 8, 1892, January 29, 1913; *St. Louis Post-Dispatch*, November 1, 1890; Find A Grave, Memorial 115707202.

10. Pauline White

167. Ind. Cit., Pauline White.
168. U.S. Census, 1850, 1860; Historical Wayne County, Missouri,
169. Historical Wayne County, Missouri.
170. *OR*, Series II, 6:381.
171. Ind. Cit., Arabella White; Unfiled, Emeline White; Ind. Cit., Pauline White; Ind. Cit., T.C. White, Historical Wayne County, Missouri.
172. Confederate Records, Dekalb White; Unfiled, Pauline White.
173. Unfiled, Pauline White.
174. Ibid.; Ind. Cit., Pauline, White; CMCF, NN 2145.
175. Unfiled, Pauline White, 259041641–259041648.
176. Unfiled, Pauline White; Fellman, *Inside War*, 221. It's not certain the blanket incident involved Pauline White. Mary Pitman, a woman who'd been placed in the St. Charles Street Prison as a spy, later told about this incident, which involved a woman named White. Since Pauline was there at the same time as Pitman, the woman named White was very likely Pauline.
177. Unfiled, Pauline White; Court Martial Papers, Pauline White, Disk 2, Box 2, Folder 6, Images 4–5; CMCF, NN 2145.
178. MSPD; Ind. Cit., Pauline White.
179. Ind. Cit., Pauline White.
180. Ibid.; MSPD.
181. Historical Wayne County, Missouri; U.S. Census, 1880; *History of Southeast Missouri*, 1124.

11. Martha Cassell

182. *SLDMD*, February 6, 1864; Ind. Cit., Martha Cassell; MSPD.
183. U.S. Census, 1850, 1860.
184. Ind. Cit., Martha Cassell; Frost, *Camp and Prison Journal*, 72.
185. Ind. Cit. Martha Cassell; Ind. Cit, L.H. Rogers; Ind. Cit., Rogers; Confederate Records, L.H. Rogers.
186. Ind. Cit., Martha Cassell.
187. Ibid.
188. Ibid.
189. CMCF, NN 2141; Ind. Cit., Martha Cassell.
190. Ind. Cit., Martha Cassell.
191. Ibid.
192. Ind. Cit., M. Cassell.
193. Ind. Cit., Martha Cassell.
194. CMCF
195. Ibid.
196. MSPD; CMCF, NN 2141.
197. CMCF, NN 2141.
198. MSPD; CMCF, NN 2141.
199. MSPD; Haynes Papers, M.C. letter, dated February 7; Missouri Marriages; U.S. Census, 1870.

12. Missouri Wood

200. U.S. Census, 1850, 1860; *Keemle's St. Louis Directory*, 57. Green, *St. Louis City Directory*, 1847.
201. Two or More, F1608, Frames 441–67; Ind. Cit., Missouri Wood; Ind. Cit., Missouri Woods.
202. Ind. Cit., Missouri Wood; Two or More, F1608, Frames 441–67.
203. Ind. Cit., Missouri Wood.
204. *OR*, Series II, 7:236.
205. Ind. Cit., Missouri Woods.
206. Ibid.
207. Ibid.
208. Ibid.
209. Ibid.
210. Ind. Cit., Missouri Wood; Ind. Cit., Elizabeth Newcomer; U.S. Census, 1860.

211. Ind. Cit., Missouri Wood.
212. Two or More, F1625, Frame 410; *SLDMR*, October 22, 1864; Ind. Cit, Margaret E. Dickson; "Order of American Knights"; Ind. Cit., Missouri Wood.
213. Ind. Cit., Missouri Wood; Ind. Cit., William T. Dickson.
214. U.S. Census, 1870; *St. Louis Globe-Democrat*, November 19–20, 1878.
215. U.S. Census, 1880; Find A Grave, Memorial #179484305.

13. Emily Weaver

216. U.S. Census, 1850, 1860; Ind. Cit., Emma Weaver; Crowley, "Ordeal of Emily Weaver," 3.
217. Ind. Cit., Emma Weaver.
218. Crowley, "Ordeal of Emily Weaver," 9–10.
219. Ind. Cit., Emma Weaver.
220. Ibid.
221. Ind. Cit., Emma Weaver; CMCF, NN 2959.
222. Ind. Cit., Emma Weaver; CMCF, NN 2959.
223. Ind. Cit., Emma Weaver; U.S. Census, 1860.
224. Ind. Cit., Emma Weaver; CMCF, NN 2959.
225. Ind. Cit., Emma Weaver.
226. Ibid.
227. Ibid
228. Ibid.
229. Ibid.
230. Ibid.
231. Ibid.
232. Ibid.
233. CMCF, NN 2959.
234. Crowley, "Ordeal of Emily Weaver," 13–14.
235. Curran, *Women Making War*, chapter 6; CMCF, NN 2959.
236. Ind. Cit., Emma Weaver.
237. Ibid.
238. Ibid.; CMCF, NN 2959.
239. Ind. Cit., Emma Weaver.
240. Crowley, "Ordeal of Emily Weaver," 15–16.
241. Ibid., 16–17; CMCF, NN 2959.
242. *SLDMD*, August 2, 1864, November 18, 1864.

243. CMCF, NN 2959; Crowley, "Ordeal of Emily Weaver," 19.
244. CMCF, NN 2959.
245. Ibid.
246. Ind. Cit., Emma Weaver; *SLDMD*, November 18, 1864; Crowley, "Ordeal of Emily Weaver," 26, 30; CMCF, NN 2959.
247. Ind. Cit., Emma Weaver; Ind. Cit., Emily E. Weaver.
248. Ind. Cit., Missouri Wood.
249. *Davenport (IA) Morning Democrat*, September 30, 1864; *SLDMD*, November 18, 1864; Haynes papers, Martha Cassell letter, dated February 7.
250. *SLDMD*, November 18, 1864; Crowley, "Ordeal of Emily Weaver," 37. Rosecrans's order that Emily be released from prison suggests that she might have been recaptured prior to the promulgation of her sentence, but there seems to be no other evidence to support this supposition.
251. King, *Tilley Treasure*, 105, 145.
252. Crowley, "Ordeal of Emily Weaver," 44–45.

14. Jane Hancock

253. U.S. Census, 1850, 1860; "Denton-Herndon Family Genealogy"; Unfiled, Jane Hancock.
254. U.S. Census, 1860; Unfiled, Jane Hancock.
255. Unfiled, Jane Hancock.
256. Ibid.
257. Unfiled, Jane Hancock; Two or More, F1620, Frame 272.
258. Frost, *Camp and Prison Journal*, 170. Although there was a separate building on Gratiot Street for female prisoners by this stage of the war, some were still held in the main Gratiot Street Prison in quarters separated from the male population.
259. Frost, *Camp and Prison Journal*, 171; "Gratiot Street Prison."
260. Unfiled, Jane Hancock.
261. Ibid.
262. Ind. Cit., Jane Hancock. It's unclear whether the bill of sale in Jane Hancock's file accompanied the citizens' petition on her behalf, because the date on the bill of sale appears to be after the period of time in question.
263. Unfiled, Jane Hancock; Ind. Cit., Jane Hancock; *SLDMR*, October 3, 1864.
264. U.S. Census, 1870, 1880.

15. Kate Beattie

265. *SLDMR*, May 3, November 21, 1864.
266. Wood, "Christmas Day Massacre"; Lincoln, *Collected Works*.
267. Lincoln, *Collected Works*; *SLDMR*, November 21, 1864.
268. *SLDMR*, November 21, 1864; Shiras and Wolf, "Major Wolf and Abraham Lincoln," 357.
269. *SLDMR*, November 21, 1864.
270. Ibid.
271. Ibid.
272. Ibid.
273. Ibid.; Frost, *Camp and Prison Journal*, 195.
274. *SLDMR*, November 21, 1864.
275. Ibid.
276. Lincoln, *Collected Works*.
277. Shiras and Wolf, "Major Wolf and Abraham Lincoln," 357; Arkansas Marriages.
278. Unfiled, Maria Ackrell; Ind. Cit., E.M. Ackrell; CMCF, NN 3520.
279. Kate Beattie, Court Martial Papers, Disk 1, Box 1, Folder 6, Images 76–77; CMCF, NN 3520.
280. CMCF, NN 3520.
281. Ibid.
282. Ibid.
283. Ibid.
284. Ibid.
285. Kate Beattie, Court Martial Papers, Disk 1, Box 1, Folder 6, Images 76–77; Lincoln, *Collected Works*; *Nashville (TN) Daily Union*, January 24, 1865.
286. Unfiled, Kate Beattie; Two or More, F1101, Frame #435.
287. Ind. Cit., Beattie.
288. Shiras and Wolf, "Major Wolf and Abraham Lincoln," 57.

16. Amanda Cranwill

289. Ind. Cit., S. Cranwell; Louisiana Parish Marriages; *SLDMD*, September 9, 1858; U.S. Census, 1850, 1860; Richardson, *Scattered Leaves*; CMCF, NN 3355.
290. Ind. Cit., S. Cranwell; Ind. Cit., Amanda Cranwell; CMCF, NN3355.

291. Ind. Cit., Amanda Cranwell; Ind. Cit., A. Cranwell; Ind. Cit., A. Cranville; *SLDMR*, December 5, 1863; U.S. Census, 1860.
292. Ind. Cit., Amanda Cranville; Ind. Cit., Amanda Cranwell; Ind. Cit., A. Cranville; CMCF, NN 3355.
293. Ind. Cit., A. Cranville; *SLDMD*, Dec. 1, 1864; Ind. Cit., Amanda Cranwell.
294. *SLDMD*, Dec. 1, 1864.
295. Ind. Cit., Amanda Cranwell; CMCF, NN 3355.
296. Ind. Cit., Cranville.
297. Ind. Cit., S. Cranwell.
298. Ibid.
299. CMCF, NN 3355.
300. Unfiled, A. Cranwill.
301. *SLDMD*, January 20, 1865; CMCF, NN 3355.
302. *Memphis Bulletin*, May 27, 1865.
303. *Louisville (KY) Daily Courier*, Jun. 9, 1866; "Franklin Female College"; *Louisville (KY) Courier-Journal*, August 23, 1866, June 13, 1906; *Clarksville (TN) Chronicle*, June 28, 1873; Richardson, *Scattered Leaves*.

17. Mary Jane Duncan

304. Two or More, F1634, Frames 818–42.
305. U.S. Census, 1850, 1860; Missouri Marriages.
306. Two or More, F1634, Frames 818–42.
307. Ibid., Frames 845–56
308. Two or More, F1634, Frame 821; Ind. Cit., Mary Duncan; Unfiled, Mary Duncan.
309. Unfiled, Mary J. Duncan.
310. Ind. Cit., Mary J. Duncan; Ind. Cit., Mary Jane Duncan.
311. Unfiled, Mary Duncan.
312. Ibid.
313. Ibid.
314. Ind. Cit., Mary Duncan; Ind. Cit., Mary J. Duncan.
315. U.S. Census, 1880.

Epilogue

316. Richardson, *Scattered Leaves*, 19.
317. Richardson, *Scattered Leaves*.
318. Ind. Cit., S.F. Cleveland.
319. Curran, *Women Making War*, chapter 10; Richardson, *Scattered Leaves*, 19; "Reminiscences of Mrs. Lucy Nickolson Lindsay."
320. Sutherland, *Savage Conflict*, 139; Richardson, *Scattered Leaves*, 19.
321. See Beilein, *Bushwhackers*, for a discussion of the guerrilla conflict in Missouri as a household war.

Bibliography

Arkansas Marriages. Family Search. https://www.familysearch.org/search/collection/1417439.

Beilein, Joseph M. Jr. *Bushwhackers: Guerrilla Warfare, Manhood, and the Household in Civil War Missouri*. Kent, OH: Kent State University Press, 2016.

Burch, John P., as told by Harrison Trow. *Charles W. Quantrell: A True History of His Guerrilla Warfare*. Vega, TX: self-published, 1923.

Civil War Service Records—Confederate. Fold3.com.

Civil War Subversion Investigations. National Archives. Publication M797. Fold3.com.

Court Martial Case Files, 1809–1917. Records of the Judge Advocate General's Office. Record Group 153. Entry PC-29 15. National Archives, Washington, D.C.

Court Martial Papers, 1862–1877. Record Group 133. Office of the Adjutant General. Missouri State Archives. Jefferson City, Missouri.

Crowley, W.J. "The Ordeal of Emily Weaver." *Independence County Chronicle* 17 (October 1975): 1–45.

Curran, Thomas F. *Women Making War: Female Confederate Prisoners and Union Military Justice*. E-book. Carbondale: Southern Illinois University Press, 2020.

Dave Leip's Atlas of U.S. Presidential Elections. "1860 Presidential General Election Results—Missouri." https://uselectionatlas.org.

Bibliography

"Denton-Herndon Family Genealogy." https://freepages.rootsweb.com/~rayherndon/genealogy/index.htm.

Edwards, John N. *Noted Guerrillas*. St. Louis: Bryan, Brand & Company, 1877.

1852 St. Louis City Directory. St. Louis, MO: St. Louis Missouri Republican, 1852.

1854 St. Louis City Directory. St. Louis, MO: Chambers & Knapp, 1854.

Ellis, James Thornton. "1863 Civil War Diary." 2nd Missouri Cavalry C.S.A. 2ndmocavcsa.tripod.com/id4.htm.

Fellman, Michael. *Inside War: The Guerrilla Conflict in Missouri during the American Civil War*. New York: Oxford University Press, 1989.

Find A Grave. www.findagrave.com.

First Annual Report of the General Superintendent of the St. Louis Public Schools. St. Louis, MO: *St. Louis Republican*, 1854.

"Gratiot Street Prison." *Civil War St. Louis*. http://www.civilwarstlouis.com/Gratiot/gratiot.htm.

"Gratiot Street Prisoner List: Ledger Transcription List—Women & Children Prisoners." Civil War St. Louis. http://www.civilwarstlouis.com.

Franklin Female College. KenCat Online Collections. Western Kentucky University, Bowling Green, Kentucky. https://westernkentuckyuniversity.pastperfectonline.com/archive/70BDA91C-2F4C-462A-BF48-596815211825.

Frost, Griffin. *Camp and Prison Journal*. Quincy, IL: Quincy Herald Book and Job Office, 1867.

"General Orders No. 100: The Lieber Code." Yale Law School. https://avalon.law.yale.edu/19th_century/lieber.asp.

Green, James. *St. Louis City Directory*, 1847. Washington University Online. Washington University, St. Louis, Missouri. http://repository.wustl.edu.

Grimes, Absalom. *Absalom Grimes: Confederate Mail Runner*. Edited by M.M. Quaife. New Haven, CT: Yale University Press, 1926.

Haynes, Ada Byron. Papers. Missouri Historical Society. St. Louis, Missouri.

Hereford, Lizzie M. Powell. *Prison Diary*. Columbia: State Historical Society of Missouri. https://digital.shsmo.org.

Hereford, Lizzie M. Powell (1840–1877). Papers, 1817–1880. State Historical Society of Missouri. Columbia, Missouri. https://files.shsmo.org/manuscripts/columbia/C4152.pdf.

Historical Wayne County, Missouri. Facebook, January 27, 2018. www.facebook.com.

History of Clinton County, Missouri. St. Joseph, MO: National Historical Company, 1881.

History of Southeast Missouri. Chicago: Goodspeed Publishing Company, 1888.

History of St. Louis County. Vol. 1. Wm. L. Thomas. St. Louis, MO: S.J. Clarke Publishing Company, 1911.

Jones, Nancy Chapman. *Letters*. Cooper County (MO) Genealogy. cooper.mogenweb.org/Military/Jones_Letters.pdf.

Keemle's St. Louis Directory, 1838–'39. Washington University Online. Washington University, St. Louis, Missouri. http://repository.wustl.edu.

King, James B., Jr. *The Tilley Treasure*. Point Lookout, MO: School of the Ozarks Press, 1984.

Lincoln, Abraham. *Collected Works*. Vol. 8. Ann Arbor: University of Michigan Digital Library Production Services, 2001. http://name.umdl.umich.edu.

Louisiana Parish Marriages, 1837–1957. Family Search. https://www.familysearch.org.

Lowry, Thomas P. *Confederate Heroines*. Baton Rouge: Louisiana State University Press, 2006.

Missouri Marriages, 1750–1920. Family Search. https://www.familysearch.org.

Missouri State Penitentiary Database. Missouri State Archives. Jefferson City. https://s1.sos.mo.gov.

Moore, M.M. "Corrections of Two Articles." *Confederate Veteran* 17, no. 11 (November 1909): 40.

Nichols, Bruce. *Guerrilla Warfare in Civil War Missouri*. Vol. 2, 1863. Jefferson, NC: McFarland & Company, 2007.

Official Army Register of Volunteer Forces of the United States Army for the Years 1861, '62, '63, '65. Washington, DC: Government Printing Office, 1865–1867. https://archive.org/stream/cu31924092911134/cu31924092911134_djvu.txt.

"Order of American Knights." The Civil War in Missouri. http://www.civilwarmo.org.

Pinnell, Eathan Allen. *Serving with Honor: The Diary of Captain Eathan Allen Pinnell*. Edited by Michael E. Banasik. Iowa City, IA: Camp Pope Bookshop, 1999.

Richardson, Amanda Cranwill. *Scattered Leaves: Poems from a Collection of Poems Lost during the War*. Louisville, KY: John P. Morton & Company, 1895.

Shiras, Frances, and E.C. Wolf. "Major Wolf and Abraham Lincoln: An Episode of the Civil War." *Arkansas Historical Quarterly* 2 (1943): 353–58. Accessed February 5, 2021.

Slave Schedule, 1850, 1860. Family Search. https://www.familysearch.org.

Snead, Thomas L. *The Fight for Missouri*. New York: Charles Scribner's Sons, 1886.

St. Louis Board of Education Annual Report. St. Louis, MO: *St. Louis Republican*, 1854.

St. Louis Board of Education Annual Report. Vols. 20–21. St. Louis: Democrat Litho and Printing, 1875–76.

Sutherland, Daniel E. *A Savage Conflict: The Decisive Role of Guerrillas in the American Civil War*. Chapel Hill: University of North Carolina Press, 2009.

Thomas, William L. *History of St. Louis County*. Vol. 1. St. Louis, MO: S.J. Clarke Publishing, 1911.

Unfiled Papers and Slips Belonging in Confederate Compiled Service Records. Fold3.com.

Union Provost Marshal Papers, Two or More Civilians: 1861–1867. Missouri State Archives, Jefferson City. https://www.sos.mo.gov.

Union Provost Marshals' File of Papers Relating to Individual Citizens. National Archives Publication M-345. Fold3.com.

United States Census Records, 1850, 1860, 1880, 1900. Family Search. https://www.familysearch.org.

Violette, Eugene Morrow. *A History of Missouri*. 1918. Reprint, Cape Girardeau, MO: Ramfre Press, 1960.

The War of the Rebellion: A Compilation of the Official Records of the Union and Confederate Armies. Washington, DC: Government Printing Office, 1880–1901.

Women of Missouri in the Civil War. 1920. E-book Reprint, n.p.: Big Byte Books, 2014.

Wood, Larry. "Christmas Day Massacre." Ozarks and Missouri History. http://ozarks-history.blogspot.com/2008/12/christmas-day-massacre.html.

INDEX

A

Ackrell, Maria 112
Allen, R.C. 113, 120, 121
Alton, Illinois 44, 45, 46, 67, 70
Alton Military Prison 44, 45, 111
Atterbury, Nancy 123
Auburn, Missouri 60, 61, 62

B

Bagwill, Augusta 27, 28, 29, 30, 31
Bagwill, James 27, 31, 113
Bagwill, Zaidee 27, 28, 29
Baker, James H. 36, 57, 124
Bartholow, Thomas 60, 61, 63
Bates, Edward 85
Batesville, Arkansas 93, 94, 96, 97, 98, 99, 101, 102, 103
Battle of Hartville 44
Baxter, Elisha 102

Beattie, Kate 109, 110, 111, 112, 113, 115, 116, 121
Bellefontaine Cemetery 65, 71, 92
Bell, John 13
Blennerhassett, Edward 66
Blennerhassett, Harman 66
Blennerhassett, Richard 66
Blennerhassett, Therese 66, 67, 69, 71, 72
Blunt, James G. 63
Bray, Andrew 122
Breckinridge, John C. 13
Broadhead, James O. 64, 67, 100, 101, 128
Brooke, Eliza 58
Brooke, William B. 57, 58
Bryant, Polly Ann 104, 105
Buel, James T. 18
Bull, Eliza 96
Burbridge, John Q. 46, 47, 48
Burr, Charles 94
Burr, Edwin 94, 100, 102

Index

Burr, Nancy 93
Byrnes, Mary 54

C

Cairo, Illinois 34, 102, 104, 107
Camp Jackson 14, 40, 66
Camp Jackson Affair 15
Carondelet, Missouri 95, 96
Carthage, Missouri 15
Cassell, John F. 79
Cassell, Martha 79, 80, 81, 82, 83, 85, 87, 88, 102
Charleston, Missouri 104, 105
Chestnut Street Female Prison 33, 40, 53, 55
Clayton, Joseph 44, 45, 46
Clayton, Teresa 44, 46, 48
Cleveland, Jane 60, 61, 63
Cleveland, John 60
Cleveland, Mary S.F. 60, 61, 63, 64, 65, 128
Columbia, Missouri 80
Columbus, Mississippi 34, 40
Conditional Unionists 13, 15
Confederate army 15, 16, 30, 32, 33, 35, 40, 46, 51, 52, 60, 66, 67, 73, 81, 86, 99, 107
Coring, Augustus 117, 119, 120
Cottrill, Lizzie 89
Cox, Sarah 19
Cranwill, Amanda 116, 117, 118, 120, 121, 127, 128, 129
Cranwill, Samuel 116, 120
Creath, Jacob 22, 25
Creath, Maggie 21, 22, 23, 24, 25, 128
Crittenden, Thomas T. 38

Crumm, John 117, 118, 119, 120
Curtis, Samuel R. 25, 26, 30, 33

D

Darr, Joseph, Jr. 69, 91, 102, 107, 108, 110, 113, 114, 117
Davis, C.W. 124
Davis, Jefferson 40, 44, 45, 102
Deal, Henry 105
Dick, Franklin A. 39, 45, 46, 54
Dickson, William T. 90, 91
Dodge, Grenville M. 70, 114, 121, 123, 124
Dodge, Isaac C. 91, 99, 100
Dorsey, Caleb 57, 58
Dougherty, J.H. 46
Douglas, Stephen 13
Douthitt, Nannie 70
Doyle, Mary 86, 87, 89, 90, 92
Dryden, John D.S. 85
Dudley, G.T. 113
Duncan, Elizabeth 122, 123
Duncan, James 122
Duncan, Jonathan Marion 122
Duncan, Mary Jane 122, 123, 124, 125
Dwight, James 65

E

Eaton, Lucien 54, 69, 107
Enrolled Missouri Militia 22, 57, 60
Ewing, Thomas, Jr. 102

Index

F

Federal army 13, 15
Fisk, Clinton 74
Flanigan, J.M. 28, 30
Fletcher, Thomas 77
Fogg, Josiah 35
Foster, Samuel 115
Fredericktown, Missouri 122, 123
Frost, Daniel M. 40
Frost, Griffin 70, 71, 105, 106, 111
Frost, Lily 40
Fugate, James 105
Furguson, Margaret 123

G

Gantt, Thomas 19
Gratiot Street Female Prison 70, 118, 123, 124, 128
Gratiot Street Prison 27, 39, 52, 55, 70, 74, 79, 105, 111, 113, 114, 120, 125
Greenville, Missouri 73, 75, 77, 78
Grimes, Absalom 29, 32, 39, 51, 52, 53, 54, 55, 56, 57, 58
Guitar, Odon 38

H

Haller, George Washington 17, 18
Haller, Jacob 17
Haller, Jane 17, 19, 20
Haller, William 17, 18, 19, 20
Hancock, Henderson 104

Hancock, Jane 104, 105, 106, 107, 108
Hancock, Rebecca 104
Hannibal, Missouri 21, 24, 25, 26
Hardaway, Henry 44, 45
Haynes, Addie 32, 33, 34, 35, 36, 40, 43, 66, 82, 85, 102
Haynes, Christopher 32
Hereford, Alfred 26
Hicks, Mary E. 55, 56
Hildebrand, Sam 123
Howard, Catherine 36
Huntsville, Missouri 60
Hyssong, John 19, 20

I

Independence, Missouri 17, 18, 19, 20

J

Jackman, Sidney 38, 39, 40
Jackson, Claiborne F. 14, 15

K

Kauffman, Charles 44
Kerr, William 18, 19
Ketchum, Sarah 88
Ketchum, Solomon P. 86, 92
Keyser, W.A. 82
King, Eleanor 94, 95, 96, 97, 98
Knight, Jennie 61, 63

INDEX

L

Lexington, Missouri 15, 19, 38, 112
Lincoln, Abraham 13, 14, 20, 34, 56, 70, 85, 93, 109, 114
Lindell Hotel 95, 110
Lindsay, David H. 37, 38, 40, 41
Lingow, Belle 96
Lingow, Laura Belle 95, 98
Lingow, Mary Jane 95, 98
Loan, Ben 19
Lost Cause, myth of the 128, 129
Louden, Mary 39, 40
Luckett, William F. 28, 29, 30, 31
Luyties, D.R. 82
Lyon, Nathaniel 14, 15, 37

M

Macon, Missouri 22, 27, 29
Martin, Annie B. 66, 67, 69, 70, 71, 72
Masterson, William 39
McCammot, Sarah 86
McClellan, William 101
McKean, T.J. 26
McKinney, T.J. 46
McLure, Margaret 29, 33, 40, 43, 46
McMurtry, James 77
McPherson, Edward 20
Memphis, Tennessee 34, 40, 46, 49, 56, 63, 89, 93, 94, 96, 97, 98, 99, 101, 112, 117
Meridian, Mississippi 34, 117
Merrill, Lewis 22, 24, 25, 26
Mexico, Missouri 22

Mississippi River 34, 40, 46, 56, 70, 74, 90, 104
Missouri State Guard 15, 37, 80
Missouri State Penitentiary 73, 76, 77, 83
Mobile, Alabama 34, 46
Murrell, W.H. 69
Myrtle Street Prison 46, 51, 80, 96

N

Newcomer, Elizabeth 90
Newland, William 25
New Orleans, Louisiana 87, 116
New York, New York 36
Nicholson, Gettie 38, 39
Nicholson, Lucie 37, 38, 39, 40, 41, 42, 43, 46, 47, 129

O

Oliver Street Hotel 113
Order of American Knights 87, 91, 100

P

Palmyra, Missouri 21, 22, 23, 79
Parker, B.F. 52
Parker, Elmisa 54, 55, 56
Patrick, William K. 45, 54, 56, 57
Patterson, Missouri 74, 75
Penick, William R. 19
Pickering, Lizzie 52, 55
Pilot Knob, Missouri 74, 75, 94, 96, 100, 101, 111, 123

Index

Pitman, Mary Ann 99, 100, 101, 102
Pope, John 76, 77
Poston, Drury 74, 75, 76
Powell, Lizzie 21, 22, 24, 25, 26
Pozzoni, Carlotta 117, 119
Price, Clay 21
Price, Sterling 15, 29, 38, 39, 40, 58, 67, 71, 111
Price, T.D. 26
Priest, John W. 79, 80, 81

Q

Quantrill, William 17, 18

R

Rainwater, Hannah 49
Rayburn, Mary 96
Reed, Isaac Newton 103
Reeves, Timothy 74, 76, 109
Reid, James A. 104, 105
Reynolds, Willis M. 63, 64, 65, 128
Ribble, H.H. 96, 98
Riley, Frank 101
Rogers, Lewis (alias F.M. Kaylor) 80, 81, 82, 83
Rolla, Missouri 94, 95, 96, 97, 100
Rosecrans, William 35, 36, 57, 69, 70, 83, 87, 88, 89, 93, 102, 103, 108, 109, 110, 114, 117

S

Sanderson, John 35, 36, 56, 57, 82, 83, 87, 98, 99, 100, 102

Santa Fe, Missouri 21
Sappington, Drusella 55
Schofield, John M. 54
Scott, Nellie 89, 90
Sevier, Sarah 19, 20
Shattuck, W.C. 123
Shelby, Joseph Orville "Jo" 94, 97, 100, 102
Shepherd, James 98
Sites, John E. 87, 89, 90
Smart, Edwin 22
Snodgrass, Harriet "Hattie" 43, 44, 45, 46, 47, 48, 49, 50, 51, 54, 55
Snodgrass, Jane 48
Squire, Mary 79, 81
St. Charles Street Female Prison 34, 35, 69, 81, 90, 91, 93, 96, 99
St. Louis Daily Missouri Democrat 47, 79, 101, 118
St. Louis Daily Missouri Republican 40, 66
St. Louis, Missouri 14, 19, 25, 26, 27, 28, 31, 32, 33, 34, 36, 39, 40, 42, 43, 44, 46, 47, 48, 49, 50, 51, 52, 53, 54, 55, 56, 57, 58, 60, 61, 63, 65, 66, 67, 69, 70, 71, 74, 75, 78, 79, 80, 81, 82, 83, 86, 87, 89, 92, 94, 95, 96, 98, 99, 100, 101, 102, 105, 107, 109, 114, 115, 116, 117, 119, 120, 123, 124, 127, 129
Strachan, William 22, 24, 25
Surratt, Mary 93
Swander, R.M. 33, 44, 45, 63

T

Tallon, Peter 102, 110
Tandy, David 82
Thompson, Philip 19
Tilley, Wilson L. 93, 94, 95, 96, 97, 98, 100, 103
Todd, George 18
Troy, Missouri 61
Tuscumbia, Missouri 80

U

Union army 15, 61, 67, 93, 105

V

Vail, Cora 51, 58
Vail, Corra 51, 54, 56, 57, 58
Vail, Marion 51, 52, 53, 54, 55, 56, 57, 58, 59, 63, 136
Vail, Owen 51
Vandewater, Lewis 44

W

Wallace, Harriet 123, 124
Wallace, William 124
Walsh, Michael 113
Weaver, Abram 93, 100, 102
Weaver, Emily 90, 91, 93, 94, 96, 97, 98, 99, 100, 101, 102, 103, 128
Weaver, Mary 93
White, Arabella 73, 74
White, Dekalb 74, 76
White, Evaline 74, 77
White, Pauline 73, 74, 75, 76, 77, 78, 83, 85
White, Terrell C. 73, 74
Wilhite, James 39
Wilson, James 109, 111
Wilson's Creek, Battle of 15
Windsor, Canada 90, 91
Winer, John M. 44, 45, 46
Wolf, Enoch 109, 110, 111, 112, 113, 114, 115
Wood, Edward 86
Wood, Missouri 82, 86, 87, 88, 89, 90, 91, 92, 93, 102, 103

About the Author

The author of eight other books with The History Press, Larry Wood is a retired public school teacher and a freelance writer.

Visit us at
www.historypress.com